OPPORTUNITIES

W9-BVE-485

13.95

Allied Health Careers

OPPORTUNITIES

in

Allied Health Careers

REVISED EDITION

ALEX KACEN

McGraw·Hill

New York   Chicago   San Francisco   Lisbon   London   Madrid   Mexico City
Milan   New Delhi   San Juan   Seoul   Singapore   Sydney   Toronto

The *McGraw-Hill* Companies

Library of Congress Cataloging-in-Publication Data

Kacen, Alex.
    Opportunities in allied health careers / Alex Kacen. — Rev. ed.
        p.   cm.
    ISBN 0-07-143847-5
    1. Allied health personnel—Vocational guidance—United States.
  2. Paramedical education—United States.   I. Title.

    R697.A4K315   2005
    610.69—dc22   2004022338

Copyright © 2005 by The McGraw-Hill Companies, Inc. All rights reserved. Printed in the United States of America. Except as permitted under the United States Copyright Act of 1976, no part of this publication may be reproduced or distributed in any form or by any means, or stored in a database or retrieval system, without the prior written permission of the publisher.

1 2 3 4 5 6 7 8 9 0   DOC/DOC 0 9 8 7 6 5

ISBN 0-07-143847-5

Interior design by Rattray Design

McGraw-Hill books are available at special quantity discounts to use as premiums and sales promotions, or for use in corporate training programs. For more information, please write to the Director of Special Sales, Professional Publishing, McGraw-Hill, Two Penn Plaza, New York, NY 10121-2298. Or contact your local bookstore.

This book is printed on acid-free paper.

Contents

A case study. Allied health paraprofessional defined.
Criteria for being in an allied health career. Overview
of the health care field.

Shortage of health care workers. The solution to the
problem. Allied health workers in demand.
Government recognition and support. A word of
caution.

Introduction

INCREASINGLY, PEOPLE ARE interested in receiving preventive health care and care that not only treats medical problems, but also addresses the spiritual and psychological effects of disease. In addition, today's physicians are practicing more specialized medicine. This is where allied health care comes in. Allied health care is composed of a wide range of health and medical career paths and includes a variety of practitioners who work together to ensure the health of the whole person. The goal of those practicing integrated medicine is to help people become and remain healthy in all aspects of their lives.

Allied health careers involve professionals and paraprofessionals who are qualified by special training, education, skills, and experience to provide a wide range of health care services and treatment. Paraprofessionals work under the supervision of or in collaboration with a licensed practitioner; paraprofessionals include, but are not limited to, physician assistants, licensed practical nurses, certified nurse assistants, home health aides, radiological technologists and technicians, medical therapists, and other qualified technologists and technicians.

In this book you will read about paraprofessionals working in a range of occupations that provide some assistance to or work in collaboration with a licensed professional, such as a medical doctor or a registered nurse. (If you are interested in learning about professional career paths not discussed in this book, you should search your local library or an online bookstore for the appropriate title in the *Opportunities in* . . . series of books.) Each chapter in this book presents a different category of allied health professional—from medicine and nursing to dentistry and eye care. Within each chapter, you will read about specific job requirements and responsibilities for each career, training and education required to enter the field, any certification requirements, earnings, and opportunities for employment. Also, be sure to peruse the Appendix at the back of the book. In it, you'll find a list of associations and organizations—and their websites—that you can contact or look up for additional information.

Whether as an emergency medical technician, paramedic, dental assistant, or physical therapy assistant, if you are interested in pursuing a career in allied health care, you need to have one special characteristic: a genuine desire to help people. Coupled with compassion and a respect for life, that desire grows and fosters wonderful opportunities for you to care for patients in need. Don't be surprised if you learn something about yourself along the way as well.

As you consider your career choice, look carefully and closely not just at the choices in front of you, but also at the qualities and desires within you. Only then will you know if you are making the right choice. And to those who choose health care, welcome to the team!

1

WHAT IS AN ALLIED
HEALTH CAREER?

ONLY ABOUT ONE-THIRD of the health care workers providing patient care today are doctors, nurses, or dentists. The other two-thirds include a variety of allied health workers, who facilitate and further clinical care through medical testing, patient education, rehabilitation services, and many other—often highly specialized—functions. The allied health professions include more than sixty disciplines that are involved with the delivery of health or related services pertaining to the identification, evaluation, and prevention of diseases and disorders; with dietary and nutrition services; and with rehabilitation and health system management. Workers in allied health are found not only in numerous health care delivery settings, such as hospitals, clinics, laboratories, and long-term care facilities, but also in business and industry.

For those who want to work in health care, but don't want to spend their young adult years in medical school—and the rest of their lives financing it—opportunities in allied health careers are exciting and numerous. In this chapter, you will read a case study that describes how an individual experiencing a stroke might receive excellent care from a number of allied health paraprofessionals, understand what the phrase "allied health paraprofessional" means, and get an overview of the field of health care.

A Case Study

It happened so quickly that Ted, a self-made businessman in his mid-fifties who ran a successful insurance agency, didn't know what hit him. He was at home relaxing on a sunny Sunday afternoon, preparing to barbecue some steaks, when suddenly he felt dizzy and was hit by a strange numbness of his right side, both arm and leg. He called out to his wife, Heather, who heard him and ran out of the house.

"What's the matter, dear?" she cried. "I don't know, but the whole right side of my body seems to be numb and I feel dizzy. Maybe I need a doctor," was Ted's reply.

Heather, whose best friend, Alice, had recently suffered a stroke, knew that Ted's symptoms resembled those of a stroke and that time was extremely important, in fact, that it could be a matter of life and death. She immediately got on the phone and dialed 911.

When the operator answered, Heather told her what had happened and asked for an ambulance to be sent immediately. Within a few minutes she heard the ambulance wail, and shortly afterwards she admitted a two-man team of emergency medical technicians to her home. Quickly, the two checked Ted's breathing, which was labored. They deftly placed him on a stretcher and positioned his head and shoulders on a pillow to help him breathe easier. Placing him in the ambulance, they proceeded to the closest hospital. Once there, they rushed Ted into the emergency room, where he was immediately examined by the attending physician.

In fact, Heather was right; Ted did have a stroke, which is a very serious medical condition. According to the American Heart Association, it's the third-largest cause of death, ranking behind "diseases of the heart" and all forms of cancer. Thanks to the quick work of the two allied health professionals, Ted was not in immediate danger of death.

Ted's attending physician first performed an arteriography to determine both the kind of stroke Ted had and the proper treatment for it. The procedure located a blockage of the artery supplying blood to the brain, known in medical terminology as an embolism.

The doctor knew that since Ted had been rushed to the hospital in a matter of minutes, he was a good candidate for the administration of TPA, a medicine known as a clot buster, which has obtained wonderful results in opening up circulation to large areas of the brain before they can become permanently damaged.

A surgeon assistant was standing by in case an emergency carotid enderectomy had to be performed. (A surgeon assistant is neither a nurse nor a physician, but a medical worker a notch or two lower than a surgeon who can perform most of the procedures of the surgeon, under a surgeon's guidance.) Carotid enderectomy has proven effective in stroke patients who have at least 70 percent blockage of the carotid artery. In such cases, the surgeon opens up the affected artery and removes the plaque blocking it.

In Ted's case, the surgeon assistant, working under the attending surgeon, handled a variety of duties very much like those done by the surgeon, thus freeing up the surgeon in charge to take care of more complex duties.

After the surgery, Ted, as part of the treatment plan, received both occupational and physical therapy. In both cases, the physical therapist and the occupational therapist were helped by special assistants. The occupational therapist assistant helped Ted to relearn the tasks involved in caring for himself—such as putting on his shoes and shirt, buttoning his shirt, clasping and tying his tie, and, in general, grooming himself as he had been doing prior to the stroke.

Afterwards, Ted was referred to a physician assistant when his own physician was out of town. The physician assistant, a knowledgeable young woman, looked and acted like a physician, and had she not introduced herself as "Monica Trimble, a physician assistant," Ted would never have known that she was not a doctor. But since Trimble had come right out and admitted that she was not a doctor, Ted could not help wondering what he had gotten himself into and why he could not see his own physician. However, his fears and concerns proved groundless as soon as he learned that not only was Trimble able to spend more time with him, she also was able to lay out a complete schedule of exercise, diet, and medication that would prove very helpful in speeding Ted's postoperative recovery over the weeks ahead.

In the case just described, we have gone into detail about a stroke suffered by a middle-aged businessman; his treatment by emergency medical technicians, who were the first on the scene; his surgery in the hospital; and his postoperative recovery and rehabilitation. Although he didn't realize it, Ted was treated by many allied health professionals during each stage of his illness: first by the EMTs in the ambulance; next by a nurse anesthetist, who worked in the hospital under the direction of the anesthesiologist who placed him under anesthesia prior to surgery; then by a surgery assistant, who acted as an assistant first-class in working with the surgeon during every phase of the surgery and handling the stitching of the wound itself; then by the occupational and physical therapy assistants, who facilitated Ted's recovery and helped him regain the full use of his arms and legs; and finally by the physician assistant, in Ted's postsurgery follow-up visits.

Allied Health Paraprofessional Defined

What exactly is an allied health paraprofessional? Most of us, for instance, know that a professional is one who by virtue of his or her education and training has acquired skills necessary for a given career. Medicine, engineering, law, accounting, and architecture are all careers that require professionally trained practitioners. To qualify for such professions, you must have at least a bachelor's degree and, in many cases, considerably more education, as in the case of medicine. To become a medical doctor, for example, you must have at least four years of undergraduate (college) work, four years of medical school, and a minimum of three years of residency (specialty) training, depending upon the field of medicine in which you choose to specialize.

Not so clear, however, is the meaning of the term *allied health paraprofessional*. To be sure, many of us have heard similar titles, such as *paramedic* (now called "emergency medical technician") or *paralegal*, but few of us really understand what these words mean, or our understanding is fragmentary and incomplete at best.

It will help to define the term *para*, which is the Greek word for "beside." The paramedical is, therefore, the one who works near or "beside" the medical professional, the physician, dentist, or optometrist. In the case of the physician assistant and licensed practical nurse, not only do they work near the physician or nurse, they perform many of the same functions of these jobs and work equally closely with patients.

Allied health is an odd term, one that does not have an exact, agreed-upon definition. Allied health paraprofessionals have been described by the American Medical Association as "a large cluster of health-related personnel who fill necessary roles in the health-care system." The most simplistic, collective usage of the phrase "allied health" is used to mean health professionals other than doctors and nurses. Thus, allied health paraprofessionals are workers who complement, extend, and otherwise support the work of doctors and other licensed health care workers, including nurses, anesthesiologists, dentists, and ophthalmologists. They work with various licensed professionals to make their jobs easier and more effective. They serve as extenders, or right-hand assistants, by enabling the doctor to render medical care or treatment to many more patients than would otherwise be possible. At the same time, they are helping to relieve the critical shortage of health care workers by taking many of the more routine chores off their shoulders and thus allowing our health care system to function more effectively.

Criteria for Being in an Allied Health Career

In this book, the phrase "allied health paraprofessional" refers to all whose work meets the following guidelines:

1. These workers have usually, but not always, completed an associate to bachelor's degree or equivalent program in their field.

2. The educational background required to qualify for the career resembles that of the profession to which it corresponds, except that it is shorter and of more limited duration. The training program of

the physician assistant, for instance, is like that of the physician, except it is not as detailed, long, or comprehensive.

3. Allied health paraprofessionals work under the supervision and guidance of the professionals they serve and to whom they are responsible. The amount of responsibility they have will depend to a great extent on their education and experience and where they work. For example, in certain rural and outlying areas of the country, physician assistants may not see their supervising physician for a week or more at a time, but they are in constant touch with their supervisors by phone or computer.

Within the parameters listed above fall such careers as physician assistants and medical assistants (both of which are two separate fields); licensed practical nurses and home health aides; ophthalmic medical assistants, technicians, and technologists; dental assistants, hygienists, and laboratory technicians; physical therapy assistants and occupational therapy assistants; podiatrist assistants; and several others, all of which will be fully described in this book.

Overview of the Health Care Field

Combining medical technology and the human touch, the health care industry administers care around the clock to millions of people—from newborns to the critically ill elderly. As the largest industry in 2002, the health care sector employed 12.9 million persons. About 16 percent of all new wage and salary jobs created between 2002 and 2012 will be in the health care field, equaling approximately 3.5 million jobs, more than in any other industry!

Health care jobs are found throughout the country, but they are generally concentrated in the largest states—in particular, California, New York, Florida, Texas, and Pennsylvania. This is because these states tend to have the highest population of people—the recipients of care. Keep in mind, however, that wherever there are people, there is the need for others to care for them, so careers in the health care field are almost always in demand no matter what the geographical location.

Nearly 518,000 establishments provide a range of health care services, varying greatly in terms of size, staffing patterns, and organizational structures. The health care industry includes small-town private practices of physicians who employ only one medical assistant, as well as busy inner-city hospitals that provide thousands of diverse jobs. Three-fourths of these establishments are offices of physicians, dentists, or other health practitioners. Although hospitals constitute only 2 percent of all health care establishments, they employ 41 percent of all workers. Almost three out of four non-hospital health care establishments employed fewer than 10 workers. By contrast, more than two out of three hospital employees were in establishments with more than 1,000 workers.

Occupations in the Health Care Industry

Health care establishments generally employ a mix of professionals, paraprofessionals, and workers in service occupations. Together, professionals and paraprofessionals account for three out of four jobs in the industry. The next largest share of jobs, 18 percent, is in office and administrative support. Management, business, and financial operations occupations account for only 5 percent of employment.

Professional occupations, such as physicians and surgeons, dentists, registered nurses, social workers, and physical therapists, usually require at least a bachelor's degree in a specialized field or higher education in a specific health care field, although registered nurses also enter through associate degree, and, less commonly, through diploma programs. As we've discussed, professional workers often have high levels of responsibility and complex duties, including supervision of other workers.

Paraprofessionals and technicians work in many fast-growing occupations, such as medical records and health information technician, nursing aide, and dental and medical assistant. These workers operate technical equipment and assist health diagnosing and treating practitioners. Graduates of one- or two-year training programs often fill such positions; the jobs usually require specific formal training beyond high school, but usually no more than four years of college. With experience and, in some cases, further education and training, these workers may advance to higher-level positions or transfer to new occupations.

Where to Work?

One of the many benefits of working in the field of health care is the flexibility you'll have in terms of where and for whom you can work. The health care industry is made up of the following major categories of work establishments:

• **Hospitals.** Hospitals provide complete medical care, including diagnostic services, surgery, and continuous nursing care. Some hospitals specialize in treatment of the mentally ill, cancer patients, or children. Hospital-based care may be on an inpatient (overnight) or outpatient basis. As hospitals work to improve efficiency, care continues to shift from an inpatient to outpatient basis whenever possible. Many hospitals have expanded into long-term and home health care services, providing a wide range of care for the communities they serve.

The mix of workers needed varies, depending on the size, geographic location, goals, philosophy, funding, organization, and management style of the institution. Hospitals employ workers with all levels of education and training, thereby providing a wider variety of services than is offered by other segments of the health services industry. About one in four hospital workers is a registered nurse. Hospitals also employ many physicians and surgeons, therapists, and social workers.

• **Outpatient care centers.** Among the diverse establishments in this group are kidney dialysis centers, outpatient mental health and substance abuse centers, health maintenance organization medical centers, and freestanding ambulatory surgical and emergency centers. Other ambulatory health care services included in this relatively small industry segment are ambulance services, blood and organ banks, pacemaker monitoring services, and smoking cessation programs. Because this industry segment includes ambulance services, it employs almost two out of every five emergency medical technicians and paramedics and a third of all ambulance drivers and attendants. In addition, this segment of the health care industry employs counselors, social workers, and nurses.

• **Medical and diagnostic laboratories.** Medical and diagnostic laboratories provide analytic or diagnostic services to the medical profession or directly to patients following a physician's prescription. Workers may analyze blood, take x-rays and computerized tomography scans, or perform other clinical tests. Professional and related workers, primarily clinical laboratory and radiologic technologists and technicians, make up about 42 percent of all jobs in this industry segment. Service workers employed in this segment include medical assistants, medical equipment preparers, and medical transcriptionists. Medical and diagnostic laboratories provide the fewest number of jobs in health services.

- **Nursing and residential care facilities.** Nursing care facilities provide inpatient nursing, rehabilitation, and health-related personal care to those who need continuous nursing care but do not require hospital services. Federal law requires nursing facilities to have licensed personnel on hand twenty-four hours a day and to maintain an appropriate level of care at all times. Other facilities, such as convalescent homes, help patients who need less assistance. Residential care facilities provide around-the-clock social and personal care to children, the elderly, and others who have limited ability to care for themselves. Workers care for residents of assisted-living facilities, alcohol and drug rehabilitation centers, group homes, and halfway houses. Nursing and medical care, however, is not the main focus of establishments providing residential care, as it is in nursing care facilities.

Paraprofessionals make up more than three out of five nursing and residential care facility jobs and include primarily nursing, psychiatric, and home health aides. Nursing aides provide the vast majority of direct care. Professional and administrative support occupations are a much smaller percentage of employment than in other parts of the health care industry.

- **Home health care services.** Skilled nursing or medical care, under a physician's supervision, is sometimes provided in the home. Home health care services are provided mainly to the elderly. The development of in-home medical technologies, substantial cost savings, and patients' preference for care in the home have helped make this once-small segment of the industry into one of the fastest growing in the economy.

More than half of all jobs in this type of establishment are paraprofessionals who are mostly home health aides and personal and home care aides. Nursing and therapist jobs also account for substantial shares of employment in the home health care area.

- **Offices of physicians.** More than a third of all health care establishments fall into this industry segment. Physicians and surgeons practice privately or in groups of practitioners who have the same or different specialties. Many physicians and surgeons prefer to join group practices because they afford backup coverage, reduce overhead expenses, and facilitate consultation with peers. Physicians and surgeons are increasingly working as salaried employees of group medical practices, clinics, or integrated health systems.

- **Offices of dentists.** About one out of every five health care establishments is a dentist's office. Most employ only a few workers, who provide general or specialized dental care, including dental surgery. Dental assistants make up about a third of all jobs in dentists' offices. The typical staffing pattern in dentists' offices consists of one dentist with a support staff of dental hygienists and dental assistants. Larger practices are more likely to employ office managers and administrative support workers.

- **Offices of other health practitioners.** This segment of the industry includes the offices of chiropractors, optometrists, podiatrists, occupational and physical therapists, psychologists, audiologists, speech-language pathologists, dietitians, and other miscellaneous health practitioners. Demand for the services of this segment is related to the ability of patients to pay, either directly or through health insurance and hospitals and nursing facilities that may contract out for these services. These offices also include those of practitioners of alternative medicine, such as acupuncturists, homeopaths, hypnotherapists, and naturopaths.

2

THE NEED FOR ALLIED HEALTH PARAPROFESSIONALS

THE SUBJECT OF health care reform has dominated the evening news and newspaper headlines for the past several years. Through all of the discussions and arguments, only one thing is certain: health care and the ways it is provided will continue to change. The current emphasis is on providing quality health services to everyone. But how can we do that when our existing system is already overtaxed as a result of an aging population, fewer health care providers, AIDS, teen pregnancies, cancer, heart disease, and an epidemic of violence? The answer, or at least a partial answer, may be contained in the pages of this book: the allied health paraprofessionals. These trained and educated workers can assist and supplement physicians and nurses in caring for the growing number of patients in need of basic health services. An expansion of the role and practice of these paraprofessionals could further improve the efficacy with which some health services are delivered. In addition, governmental legislation and funding to increase awareness of careers in the allied health field will help alleviate critical health care shortages.

Just a few decades ago, most of the careers discussed in this book did not even exist. But in a relatively short time, the demand for these careers has grown far more quickly than almost anyone could have foreseen. How could they have attained such prominence so fast? The answer lies in a complex of factors, including the shortage of primary care physicians and nurses, who build the base of health care in the United States; the growing demand for services, which can be attributed to several factors that are discussed below; and the resultant escalation of health care costs.

Shortage of Health Care Workers

The current shortage of health care workers stems from a variety of factors, yet it is beyond the scope of this book to discuss more than only a few of the most obvious reasons. The rapid emergence of HMOs (health maintenance organizations) and managed care, with its emphasis on health maintenance and disease prevention, accounts for a great deal of the current shortage in health care workers. In addition, the demand for health care services is rising as a result of an aging population. The number of workers providing health care has not been able to keep pace with the increasing number of treatment options available to a growing and aging population, resulting in an unprecedented shortage of workers in all segments of health care. The good news for those of you seeking to enter any health care field is that upon graduation you will be guaranteed a job with competitive pay.

Today, thanks to medical science and technology, people are living longer and are better able to endure the onslaught of diseases that just a few decades ago would have devastated our population.

Many of these former scourges—such as polio and diphtheria—have either been eradicated or are under control, and much progress has been made in reducing the number of deaths due to cancer and heart disease, among others. This means that people are living longer and more productive lives. The U.S. Census Bureau reports that rapid growth of the population age sixty-five and over will begin in 2011, when the first of the baby boom generation reaches age sixty-five.

Given the fact that the U.S. population is growing older, numerous factors point to a future increased demand for health care services. As the number of older persons in the population increases, so does the prevalence of chronic conditions, which will fuel a greater demand for a variety of health services and workers to provide these services. Today, it is estimated that 125 million Americans live with a chronic condition, and by 2020, as the population ages, that number will increase to an estimated 157 million, with 81 million of them having two or more chronic conditions.

General practitioners report that their training does not adequately prepare them to care for a patient experiencing several chronic conditions and expressing a variety of health care concerns requiring patient education, advice on activities of daily living, and nutritional guidance. Yet while allied health professionals can provide these aspects of care, present workforce trends suggest that some portions of the allied health community will be ill equipped to meet the expected demand for services because of personnel shortages. Legislative efforts, which will be discussed later in this chapter, are underway to address these concerns.

Fueling further demand for health care services is the fact that most of us are covered by some form of health insurance, public or private. This was not true prior to World War II, when nearly 90 percent of Americans paid for health care services out of their own pockets. Today, with increased numbers of our citizens covered by such federal programs as Medicare (for those over age 55) and Medicaid (for those living below the poverty level), as well as insurance companies like Blue Cross & Blue Shield, which covers 100 million Americans, health care is more than ever within the grasp of millions. While our parents or grandparents might have been reluctant to see a doctor or to enter a hospital unless they were desperately ill, these considerations are largely a thing of the past for those with insurance, since the government or private insurance picks up the health care bill. Today, many of us go to the doctor for relatively minor incidents. With the increase in the number of people seeking care and the way in which managed care pays (or doesn't pay) for services, the price of such services has skyrocketed and physicians and other health care professionals are receiving less reimbursement for their time and effort. This has led to physicians seeking specialty practice where they will receive top dollar for specific treatments and created the need for others to do the tasks that aren't directly reimbursed by managed care.

The rapid growth of nursing homes, birthing centers, community centers, emergency and surgicenters, and various other centers—some privately funded and some public agencies—is yet another cause for the rise in demand for health care specialists. These organizations are primarily larger and more institutional in their outlook, which means that we can expect to see a greater demand for allied health professionals to handle the more routine assignments that a doctor would have performed in private practice.

Finally, there has been a sharp upsurge in our awareness and understanding of health care services because of greater exposure by the media; newspapers, radio, TV, and the Internet are informing us about health care issues and technology. Every day we are bombarded by new discoveries to help diagnose and bring under control all manner of diseases and health conditions. As new technologies in the diagnosis and treatment of disease are announced, we are demanding these services. Accompanying this demand for medical treatment and care has been a dramatic increase in the development of new drugs, health care services, and products over the past few decades. In 2001, the United States spent $1.4 trillion on health care; this is equivalent to the amount of money the French economy produced that year. Currently, Americans spend approximately 15 percent of the gross national product on health care products and services. This is more than any other country in the world even though, as a group, Americans are no sicker than any other population.

The Solution to the Problem

In an attempt to stop runaway health care costs, the government has adopted a multifaceted program that, in its distilled form, results in shorter hospital stays and fewer admissions. Additional steps to bring down costs include prospective payments (made in anticipation of actual costs) through Diagnosis Related Groups (DRGs). Here the government pays hospitals and other health care providers just so much for a wide variety of illnesses and diagnoses. If providers can keep costs of health care services under the amount allotted in the DRGs, they can make a profit, but if costs exceed the funds allotted, the providers must absorb the additional costs. The federal government's cost-cutting efforts in turn have prompted health care providers such as hospitals, nursing homes, and private clinics to try to cut costs to an ever-increasing degree. One of the most effective ways to do this is by increasing the number of paraprofessionals who can do some of the same work of their professional counterparts at a much lower cost.

Allied health paraprofessionals were trained to handle the more routine patient care cases, thus freeing up the doctor or nurse to handle the more serious and complex problems. The physician would continue to care for seriously ill patients while the paraprofessional—in this case the physician assistant—would handle the less complex and the more routine cases. That is how the first and one of the most rapidly expanding paraprofessional careers, the physician assistant, came into being.

In the fall of 1965, conditions were right to begin a new program to train physician assistants at Duke University. The shortage of physicians was acute, and hospital and medical corpsmen who had received excellent health care training in the Korean and Vietnamese wars, were seeking out new ways to utilize their training and know-how. These corpsmen had a lot to offer and were excellent candidates to serve as clinical assistants to physicians in private practice.

From the original four corpsmen enrolled in that first class at Duke, the physician assistant program has grown, and today it encompasses approximately 10,000 students in training in 134 accredited PA programs, primarily anchored at large medical centers and universities. With the support of physician assistants, doctors have been able to see roughly 40 percent more patients. By assigning physician assistants to handle the routine and relatively simple procedures such as taking case histories and conducting physician exams, doctors have been able to reserve their knowledge for patients requiring more specialized care. In the inner city and in wide stretches of rural areas, where doctors are not so available, physician assistants and nurses have stepped up to fill the void, delivering quality health care to underserved populations.

Physician assistants can be trained at a fraction of the cost and time that it takes to train a physician, resulting in salaries that are much lower than those of the physician. This, in turn, has served as a limit on runaway health care costs. To put it another way, without the use of these allied health paraprofessionals, in this case the physician assistant, the cost of health care would be much higher.

What is true of the medical profession and the physician assistant is also true of the other allied health workers described in this book. By freeing up the more heavily trained professionals they work for—the doctor, dentist, podiatrist, advanced practice nurse, or occupational or physical therapist—to concentrate on the more serious and complex cases, paraprofessional workers have enabled the various medical professionals to handle a much greater patient load than would otherwise be possible.

Allied Health Workers in Demand

The well-being of the U.S. population depends to a considerable extent on having access to high-quality health care, which requires the presence of an adequate supply of allied health professionals. Yet, even many allied health professions are characterized by existing workforce shortages, declining enrollments in academic institutions, or a combination of both factors. For example, hospital officials have reported vacancy rates of 18 percent among radiologic technologists and 10 percent among laboratory technologists.

The American Hospital Association has identified declining enrollment in health education programs as a factor leading to critical shortages of health care professionals. In 2002, data from 90 institutions belonging to the Association of Schools of Allied Health Professions showed that, among others, the following professions have been unable to reach academic enrollment capacity: cytotechnology, dietetics, emergency medical sciences, health administration, health information management, medical technol-

ogy, occupational therapy, rehabilitation counseling, and respiratory therapy. The Bureau of Labor Statistics (BLS) states that
between the years 1998 and 2008, a total of 93,000 positions in
clinical laboratory science need filling in the form of creating
53,000 new jobs and filling 40,000 existing vacancies. Unfortu-
nately, of the 9,000-plus openings per year, academic institutions
are producing only 4,990 clinical laboratory science graduates
annually. Furthermore, accredited respiratory therapy programs in
2000 graduated 5,512 students—21 percent fewer than the 6,062
graduates in 1999. In 2001, the number of graduates from these
schools fell another 20 percent to 4,437. The BLS expects employment of respiratory therapists to grow faster than the average of all
occupations, increasing from 21 percent to 35 percent through
2010. The aging population and an attendant rise in the incidence
of not only respiratory ailments, such as asthma and chronic
obstructive pulmonary disease, but cardiopulmonary diseases as
well, drive this demand. The recent outbreak of Severe Acute Respiratory Syndrome (SARS) in other countries adds one more red
flag of worry in the event widespread infection occurs in the United
States.

Government Recognition and Support

In the 1960s, personnel shortages affected many health professions.
At that time, critical specialties, including medical technologists,
biomedical engineers, dental hygienists, and other college-trained
health workers were dangerously understaffed. These personnel,
allied with doctors, dentists, and nurses, constituted the modern
health care team; they extended the reach and the scope of the
physician. Apart from the more distinct classifications of medi-

cine—osteopathy, dentistry, veterinary medicine, optometry, podiatry, pharmacy, nursing, and public health—workers in these specialties and supportive roles lacked a common identifying name. Prior to introducing legislation to correct workforce shortages, a unifying label had to be designated for these other professions for federal support to be directed their way.

In 1966, a meeting was convened in Washington, D.C., for the purpose of producing such an identifying category. After much discussion, government officials and deans of universities where various health programs were housed were unable to come to a consensus as to what the appropriate name should be. Finally, a secretary who was taking notes at the meeting suggested that a new grouping of health professions be created called "allied health." While the secretary's name has been forgotten, the name she bestowed upon these critical members of the health care team has endured.

Legislation

On March 1, 1966, President Lyndon Johnson requested that Congress enact legislation that would deal with the problem of allied health workforce shortages. Specific goals of the legislation would be to strengthen the health care system, train needed health workers, increase research efforts, and take additional steps to meet special health problems. The President encouraged Congress to provide grants for training in allied health professions, construct and improve needed educational facilities, offer fellowships for students in advanced training, and stimulate institutions to develop new types of health personnel. The result was that President Johnson signed the Allied Health Professions Training Act into law on November 3, 1966.

Beginning with President Richard Nixon and extending through the presidencies of Gerald Ford and Jimmy Carter, the U.S. government adopted the position that it had addressed the allied health workforce problem adequately and that it was time to terminate funding. Consequently, no money was provided for allied health grant programs after 1979 until 1990, when there was, once again, a recognizable shortage of allied health workers and the need to encourage people to enter the field.

In 1990, funding for allied health grants was a mere $737,000, compared to $8 million in 1979, although funding gradually increased throughout the 1990s. Eventually, three other small grant programs (chiropractic, clinical psychology, and podiatric medicine) were combined with allied health. The 2003 appropriation for these grants was increased to $11.9 million.

In 2002, a meeting of presidents and executive directors from professional associations spanning the range of allied health careers—from dietetics to occupational therapy and from dental hygiene to clinical laboratory science—was held to discuss what additional legislation might be possible to help address shortages in the allied health fields. The gathering may be considered a first insofar as individuals at this level representing such a range of professions never had been in the same room to discuss issues that they have in common. Members of the various professional groups were interested in seeing if steps could be taken to produce legislation along the lines of the Nurse Reinvestment Act, a bill that was passed to address nurse shortages as well as the declining applications and enrollments at nursing schools. During the meeting, it was determined that this new legislative initiative should be called the Allied Health Reinvestment Act and that the Association of Schools of Allied Health Professions (ASAHP) should play the coordinating role in the pursuit of workforce legislation.

Allied Health Reinvestment Act of 2004

From the fall of 2002 to the spring of 2003, ASAHP staff worked with government legislative staff on a draft bill that went through nine iterations. Finally, the bill was ready to be forwarded to the legislative counsel's office in each chamber, where it was converted into the proper legislative language and eventually assigned House and Senate bill numbers.

The goal of the Allied Health Reinvestment Act is to increase public awareness of the different career paths in the allied health professions, highlight the advantages and rewards of those professions, and encourage individuals to enter those professions. If successful, the Allied Health Reinvestment Act of 2004 will obligate the federal government to furnish monetary support for the following activities, among others:

- Grants for national, state, and local public service announcements to attract recruits to the allied health professions
- Grants for recruitment activities in the form of outreach programs aimed at elementary and secondary schools
- Grants for allied health education, practice, and retention activities
- Student loan program for allied health faculty
- Tuition scholarships for guaranteed service in rural and other medically underserved areas
- Grants for partnerships between education programs and health care facilities

As of the fall of 2004, the bill awaits further committee discussion in both the House of Representatives and the Senate. For the current status of this bill and other government legislation, go online to http://thomas.loc.gov, type "Allied Health Reinvestment Act" into the search engine, click on the link to the bill, then the link to the bill status and summary file.

A Unified Voice in Government

The fact that people from so many disparate organizations were able to work cooperatively to produce an allied health piece of legislation is a monumental achievement. Indeed, many allied health professionals have lamented the absence of an entity at the National Institutes of Health that would direct funding specifically for allied health. A next step in the evolutionary process of the allied health field may be for several professional associations to join forces for the explicit purpose of seeking legislation to create a National Institute of Allied Health—a common voice for the many people working in the field.

A Word of Caution

The allied health field is one that is rapidly expanding and offers growth potential matched by very few other fields. Even so, a few words of caution are necessary. This may not be the right field for you. As a paraprofessional, you will be taking orders and following the instructions of the professionals under whom you work. You will be expected to follow these orders precisely or have a very good reason for deviating from them. If you have trouble taking orders from others, then you should not invest the time and money required to become a paraprofessional.

Also, while there are many examples of paraprofessionals who, with additional training and experience, have gone on to reach the level of those for whom they work, you should not regard a paraprofessional career as a stepping-stone to another professional career. For example, if you are working as a physician assistant and aspire to become a physician, you may find your credentials as a physician assistant largely worthless, and you may have to start from scratch in studying for that profession.

The best reason to enter the allied health field is because you believe it is right for you and not because it may serve as a stepping-stone to a higher paying and more prestigious job as a physician or dentist. Although paraprofessionals can and do sometimes advance into other professional ranks, it is more the exception than the rule.

Since many allied health careers are relatively new and growing fields, there is considerable flexibility in the duties you may be asked to assume. Many factors may determine what your actual workday is like: your own experience, what your supervisor thinks you should and can handle, where you work (in the inner city, for instance, or at a large metropolitan health center), and the number of patients to be seen as well as your own talents, likes, and abilities. Worth mentioning, however, is the fact that if you don't like your present situation, you can always look for the same kind of opportunity almost anywhere else in the country as the demand for jobs nationally is high.

Finally, although it is possible, don't expect to work a nine-to-five daily schedule, five days a week. If you need this kind of regularity, then perhaps you should look for another profession. Many health services establishments operate around the clock and need staff at all hours. Shift work is common in some occupations, such as with nurse assistants. Although you may not have to put in the number of hours that your supervisor does, more often than not your workdays will be long and strenuous, and they may include evening and weekend shifts. This is especially true of physician assistants and nurses as well as emergency health technicians (para-medics); patients become sick or have emergencies any hour of the day or night, seven days a week, weekends and holidays. That said, in many cases, paraprofessionals find this kind of versatility bene-ficial to them.

The good news is that the Bureau of Labor Statistics has labeled many allied health careers—including dental hygienists, physical and occupational therapy assistants, and medical assistants—among the fastest-growing occupations and those with the greatest increase in employment projected by the year 2006. While the job outlook is good for all categories of allied health careers, the demand for primary care doctors and allied health professionals in the inner city and rural areas is especially keen. This is particularly good news for those who want to make a big difference in an underserved community and those who have concerns about paying for their education.

3

EDUCATION AND TRAINING

A VARIETY OF programs after high school provide specialized training for jobs in the allied health care field. You can enter a program leading to a certificate or a degree at the associate, baccalaureate, professional, or graduate level. Two-year programs resulting in certificates or associate degrees are typically the minimum standard credential for occupations such as dental hygienist or radiologic technologist. In addition, there are many job opportunities available if you do not have the inclination or means to gain training beyond high school. In fact, more than half of the workers in nursing and residential care facilities have no greater education than a high school diploma, as do a quarter of workers in hospitals.

If you do decide to continue your education beyond high school, you'll be happy to know that educational opportunities in the allied health fields are found in a range of places, including colleges and universities, vocational and technical schools, community or junior colleges, academic health centers, hospitals, clinics, blood banks, and government institutions.

Within colleges and universities, various allied health programs may be centralized in a school of medicine, health, health sciences, health professions, or allied health. These schools are split into departments that focus on a specific career path. In colleges and universities that have a school of allied health, for example, physical therapy, nursing, health administration, and other programs of study within the allied health fields are part of the same school. In other cases, training to become a dental assistant would fall under the auspices of the dental school.

Accreditation

If you decide to pursue a degree you will want to choose allied health programs within an institution that is regionally or nationally accredited. Some legitimate allied health programs do not have institutional accreditation (particularly programs that do not award a degree and that are offered in hospitals and other nonacademic settings). This means that the institution as a whole is not accredited. If you are considering such a program, you should look into possible problems related to state approval status and weigh other quality measures with particular care.

Each allied health educational program participates in an ongoing process of self-analysis and is required to meet specific criteria or standards of accreditation. Accreditation is designed to ensure that programs are following nationally accepted norms of quality in the curriculum and educational processes they employ. Professional accreditation involves a periodic review of each program that includes a visit to the program by trained site evaluators.

In addition to institutional accreditation, professional accreditation has been established in almost all allied health fields. Again, you should verify that the program you are considering is professionally accredited (if a professional accrediting body does exist for the field). Professional accreditation generally plays a more important role in allied health areas than in most other fields of study. If you are considering a program that is not professionally accredited, you need to be aware of how this could affect your future state licensure, professional certification or registration, and, if you are an international student, your home country recognition of the credential.

The largest accrediting body for allied health programs is the Commission on Accreditation of Allied Health Education Programs (CAAHEP), an umbrella organization that incorporates a number of agencies for different fields. CAAHEP currently accredits approximately 1,700 programs in more than 1,000 institutions and 18 allied health disciplines. In addition, by reviewing the websites of professional organizations and associations for your area of interest, you should be able to find a list of accredited schools (see the Appendix).

Levels of Study

A nondegree, hospital-based apprenticeship was the first type of preparation offered for most allied health careers. This type of program still exists and remains a major career entry path in some allied health fields, such as dental laboratory technology or electrocardiograph technology. However, because job responsibilities have become more complex, the majority of allied health careers today require some formal college training. Educational opportunities beyond the bachelor's degree tend to be required for allied health professions. Because this book is focusing on allied health paraprofessional careers, we won't be discussing education beyond the bachelor's degree.

Associate Degree and Vocational Certificate

A two-year associate degree or even a one-year vocational certificate alone is sufficient preparation to enter many allied health careers. In other cases, you may attend a community college for its first two years of study (because of low tuition, open admissions, or other reasons), then continue elsewhere after earning an associate degree to complete the last two years of the bachelor's degree that you need for your chosen career.

In general, the degree titles Associate of Arts (A.A.) or Associate of Science (A.S.) indicate that degree credits may transfer toward a bachelor's degree. The Associate of Applied Science (A.A.S.) as well as certificates generally will not transfer; they are vocational credentials, indicating that the graduate has mastered the technical skills needed for a particular career. If you are considering transferring from a two-year to a four-year college, you should discuss what you need to do to transfer and what agreements the two-year college has with other four-year institutions before you even enter the two-year program.

A few of the allied health careers for which an associate degree alone is adequate preparation for career entry include dental assistants, emergency medical technicians, medical assistants, occupational therapy assistants, and physical therapy assistants.

Bachelor's Degree

The first two years of an allied health undergraduate program, like the first years of study in other majors, involves building a broad base of knowledge in the humanities, sciences, and social sciences as well as pursuing introductory prerequisites related to your chosen major. The last two years tend to focus on more specialized instruction in the major. In some cases, you must apply for admission to an allied health program after a given period of initial general study because of the major's special demands and because more students may be interested in the major than the program can support.

Allied health study adds one element to the curriculum not found in most other majors. In addition to classroom study, clinical experience in a health care setting is crucial. Extensive, supervised experience in a hospital or other clinical arena will be required for successful completion of the program.

Most bachelor's degree programs in allied health fields award the Bachelor of Science (B.S.) degree or a specialized title such as Bachelor of Physical Therapy (B.P.T.).

Master's Degree

Few of the allied health paraprofessional careers discussed in this book offer education at the master's degree level. That said, there are some that do, including the physician and pathologist assistants. This is due, in large part, to the high levels of responsibility the job carries. To enter a master's program, you must already have a bachelor's degree and will probably need some science prerequisite classes, either already contained in your degree or taken subsequently; individual programs vary in their admissions requirements. Master's programs are usually twenty-four months in duration and often provide a higher level of academic study. Included may be numerous hours of clinical study.

Entry Choices

To divide allied health career preparation into distinct levels of study may be somewhat misleading. These are young professions, with work responsibilities and educational requirements that are still evolving. In many cases, a student planning to enter a particular allied health field has a choice regarding the level of education to complete.

In cases like this, it is important to examine what the longer programs offer that the shorter ones do not. Some directors of shorter programs will expect applicants to have experience in a related profession and prior health care knowledge, or they may expect applicants to have either a bachelor's degree in another area or some other prior introductory and liberal arts study. By contrast, sometimes shorter programs have a more vocational focus, meaning that they cannot later be applied toward further academic study.

Before determining which program you should choose, ask yourself where the particular field you are interested in is going. For example, in some fields, associate's degree–level entry into the profession is being phased out. You will need to examine whether one credential may be more desirable to potential employers than the other and whether one may prepare you for additional future responsibilities.

In addition to different career paths leading to the same profession, many allied health areas involve related and similar-sounding careers: for example, the dietetic technician and the dietitian, the physical therapy assistant and the physical therapist. Students need to be aware that the educational paths for these related fields are in many cases quite separate, and that it may not be easy to move from one career to the other. Assistant-level or technician-level study may not transfer at all to other related professions because it is based in practice and technique rather than theoretical knowledge.

Admissions Requirements

According to the U.S. Department of Labor, allied health professions are hot employment areas. Seven of the top ten fastest-growing professions in the country are health fields (chiropractic medicine, counseling, respiratory therapy, speech-language pathology, occupational therapy, home health assistance, and physical therapy).

The very fact that allied health workers are in high demand, with many positions expected to open up in coming decades, has made allied health fields very popular areas of study and highly competitive fields to enter. Some institutions, particularly public institutions, give admissions preference to state residents. English fluency is also a particular concern in allied health fields because even an accent may cause difficulties in communicating with patients. Minimum TOEFL (Test of English as a Foreign Language, for those for whom English is a second language) requirements are likely to be especially high for these majors. Other tests, such as the SAT or GRE (Graduate Record Examination), are usually also required.

Another factor of special importance for applying to allied health programs is your previous experience, through work or volunteer efforts, related to health care. Admission staffs want to be sure that you understand what health care work involves because not everyone is suited to these often high-stress, low-glamour professions. Many hospitals and clinics are in great need of volunteers, and you can explore many different areas of health care through volunteer efforts, helping you to decide which career path is best for you.

Shadowing a person doing the kind of work you think you might be interested in is another way to get a better idea of what a day on the job is really like. Most people will be flattered by the interest and more than willing to answer any questions you have.

Licensure and Certification

After the completion of academic preparation, some allied health paraprofessional fields, such as the physician assistant, require graduates to earn one or more credentials prior to entering practice. Licensure is a process controlled by boards of practice operated by the governments of individual states. Requirements for licensure vary—the most common involve both demonstrating that a state-approved program of education has been completed and passing an examination. Special, limited educational licenses may be required for individuals involved in clinical care as part of an academic or training program. Licenses are requirements for practice in some allied health careers.

Professional certification or registration indicates professional competence or excellence and is awarded by professional organizations in most if not all allied health professions. The credentials awarded vary in importance from profession to profession and state to state. Certification or registration may be necessary for licensure or merely helpful for employment purposes. If you work as a podiatric assistant, for example, you may be trained on the job and not require any kind of advanced education, but your prestige on the job may be enhanced if you earn certification through the American Society of Podiatric Medical Assistants. Some organizations have both certification and registration statuses, others have one or the other, and the exact meaning often varies, which means you should do plenty of research. Requirements for certification or registration often include education, experience, and performance on examinations. In some cases, certification may be earned at the time of entry to the profession; in others, only after several years of experience. Some types of certification and registration indicate general knowledge of the profession; others indicate knowledge of a particular specialization.

Continuing Education

Almost always, allied health professionals must earn continuing education credits to maintain their licensure and professional certification or registration. These credits may be earned through actual courses, which are usually short and last only a day or so, and increasingly also through videos and other distance-education options. Conferences held by allied health professional organizations, which generally last between a few days to a week, provide a particularly good source of short training for participants. University summer schools and continuing education programs may provide additional options, and some schools of allied health can arrange special training programs for participants.

Some health care establishments provide on-the-job or classroom training, as well as continuing education. For example, in all certified nursing facilities, nursing aides must complete a state-approved training and competency evaluation program and participate in at least twelve hours of in-service education annually. Hospitals are more likely than other facilities to have the resources and incentive to provide training programs and advancement opportunities to their employees. In other segments, staffing patterns tend to be more fixed and the variety of positions and advancement opportunities more limited. Larger establishments usually offer a broader range of opportunities.

Hospitals may provide training or tuition assistance in return for a promise to work at their facilities for a particular length of time after graduation, and many nursing facilities have similar programs. Some hospitals have cross-training programs that train their workers—through formal college programs, continuing education, or in-house training—to perform functions outside their specialties, giving you an even larger cache of skills.

Paying for School

The shortage of health care workers in the industry today not only guarantees you a job upon graduation, but also means that there is a substantial amount of funding available for the education of persons entering the field. If you need financial help starting or continuing your education, as long as you invest the time and effort into looking, you'll find that financial aid is available for you from a variety of sources.

A quick online search of terms such as "financial aid," "scholarship," and "allied health" or your particular area of interest will yield a great number of websites and pages of information. A word of caution: you should never pay to have access to information about scholarships or aid money; if a website solicits you for money, it is generally not a reputable site. Instead, you should focus on sites maintained by professional associations and organizations, schools, and government agencies.

As we discussed in the previous chapter, the government is in the process of and has already passed numerous initiatives for providing scholarships and grants for people in the health professions.

For example, the Bureau of Health Professions (http://bhpr.hrsa .gov), under the auspices of the U.S. Department of Health and Human Services, offers a wealth of information for students researching health careers, including information about paying for school, scholarships, loans, and tuition assistance.

In many cases, if you are applying for federal, state, and college funds, you must meet eligibility requirements and demonstrate financial need. Special programs often have their own eligibility requirements. Student loans must be repaid after graduation or when you either stop attending school or drop below part-time status. Typically, there is a short grace period after you graduate before the first payment is due. Grants and scholarships do not need to be repaid. There are four major sources of financial aid:

- **Federal programs.** Financial aid is provided by the federal government.
- **State programs.** Financial aid is provided by the state.
- **Institutional programs.** Most colleges and schools of allied health have scholarships and grants as well as loans and work programs.
- **Special programs.** Financial aid is sponsored by community agencies, professional organizations, foundations, corporations, religious organizations, unions, clubs, and civic and cultural organizations.

If you apply for federal, state, or college aid, you must complete the Free Application for Federal Student Aid (FAFSA). This form is available at your high school or college, or you can apply online at http://fafsa.ed.gov. The FAFSA is available in January and should be completed and filed as early as possible. The application must be completed every year. Check individual school descriptions or catalogs for any school-specific preferred dates or deadlines.

Last, but not least, there are a few things you should keep in mind before you begin the process of applying for financial aid. You should have on hand all necessary financial records, including current and previous tax returns, before you begin filling out the financial aid forms. You should be sure to double check that the application is complete and that all information is accurate. Be sure to use the same name on all financial aid forms and keep copies of each completed form for your records. Monitor all mail related to financial aid and respond immediately to requests for more information, as this can be a time-consuming process and your school may have deadlines. If you think you have special circumstances that are not covered on the financial aid application, contact the college financial aid office directly. Persons working in the financial aid office are a great source of information and should be consulted if you have any questions or concerns.

4

ADVANCED PARAPROFESSIONALS IN THE MEDICAL FIELD

PHYSICIANS AND SURGEONS serve a fundamental role in our society and have an effect upon all our lives. They diagnose illnesses and prescribe and administer treatment for people suffering from injury or disease. Physicians examine patients; obtain medical histories; order, perform, and interpret diagnostic tests; and counsel patients on diet, hygiene, and preventive health care. They may use all accepted methods of treatment, including drugs and surgery to help treat disease. Physicians work in one or more of several specialties, including but not limited to anesthesiology, family and general medicine, general internal medicine, general pediatrics, obstetrics and gynecology, psychiatry, and surgery.

The medical field is a fast-paced, dynamic work environment that is sure to provide you with incredible job satisfaction. You can see the direct results of the good you do in helping people. But this is also a field in which you may experience job burnout from emotional and physical stress. If you are no stranger to hard work and possess the desire to make a real difference in a person's quality of life, this may be the area for you.

In this chapter, we focus on allied health careers that require the highest levels of training and education, usually a master's degree. Even so, this pales in comparison to the years of study and clinical practice required of those seeking their medical doctor degrees. The physician assistant, the surgical physician assistant, and the pathologist assistant are jobs with high levels of responsibility. If you think you are up to the task, read on!

Physician Assistant

As noted in Chapter 2, the physician assistant (PA) came into being primarily to help solve the acute shortage of medical manpower, particularly the primary care physician, that followed World War II, especially in the 1950s and 1960s. Unlike the medical specialist, who usually focuses on one particular disease or area of the body—such as the cardiologist who concentrates on heart disease, or the urologist who specializes in diseases of the urinary tract—the primary care physician treats the whole person, and quite often, all members of the family.

Primary care physicians are called on to care for and treat patients with a wide range of illnesses and chronic medical conditions such as diabetes or arthritis, injuries, accidents, emotional problems—in short, anything that could impair the patient's health and functioning. Under these conditions, it is clear that the physician assistant can be of great help in providing medical care and thus helping to relieve the overburdened primary care physician. Today, PA services have expanded to the point where they are working in almost all areas of medicine—specialty care as well as primary care—although primary care is still the PA's principal area of practice.

Exactly who are today's practicing physician assistants? Data from a 2003 survey by the American Academy of Physician Assistants shows that nearly 58 percent of practicing PAs are women, a number that is expected to grow as the proportion of females in PA programs also continues to rise (67 percent in 2002) and the pioneers in the field (typically male) retire. About 10 percent of the survey respondents who are clinically practicing PAs are not white. The average age of practicing PAs is 40.6 years, and the mean age of PA school graduates is 30.9 years.

It also should be noted that no allied health worker has been more closely studied or observed than the PA, and for good reason. In the past, only doctors were licensed to treat and diagnose patients' medical problems. Today, physician assistants provide medical care, including physical examinations, the ordering of appropriate tests, and the treatment of patients under the supervision of a licensed physician. Thus the PA is trained to specifically diagnose and treat an estimated 80 percent of the illnesses that are presented to the primary care physician. Referral to the physician, or close consultation between the patient, PA, and physician, is done for unusual or hard-to-manage cases. Physician assistants are taught to know when it is appropriate to refer to physicians, an important aspect of PA training. Thus, the physician has complete responsibility for the care of the patient and the PA shares in that responsibility.

What PAs Do

The scope of the PA's practice corresponds to the supervising physician's practice. PAs are licensed, registered, or certified to practice in every state (as well as the District of Columbia). Although state laws and regulations differ to some degree, these medical providers are authorized to practice medicine under the supervision of a licensed physician. PAs are able to write prescriptions for patients in forty-four states, the District of Columbia, and Guam. PAs in Arkansas and Illinois have statutory authority to prescribe and will be able to write prescriptions as soon as rules are adopted.

Physician assistants conduct physical exams, take case histories, and diagnose and treat minor illnesses or injuries. They also order lab tests and x-ray exams and interpret the results; they counsel and educate patients on good health practices. In many cases, they accompany physicians on patient rounds in both acute, short-term hospitals and in nursing homes. Other duties involve:

- Developing and putting into effect the patient management or treatment plan, recording progress notes, and assisting in providing care in the office and other outpatient facilities
- Handling such relatively simple procedures as injections, immunizations, suturing, and wound care
- Performing and noting any deviations from normal laboratory, radiological, cardiographic, and other tests to help in patient diagnosis
- Treating simple conditions produced by infection or injury and assisting in treatment of more serious illnesses, which can include helping the surgeon in performing operations and initiating diagnostic tests in response to life-threatening situations
- Referring patients to appropriate community health agencies and/or medical specialists as called for
- Educating and counseling patients in observing prescribed treatment plans dealing with such matters as normal growth

and development, problems of everyday living, family
planning, and disease prevention

Although this list is not by any means exhaustive, it does include
most of the major duties of the PA.

Training and Education

PA programs, covering both the traditional and innovative in medical education, are usually two years in length leading to a bachelor's or master's degree. All programs, in addition to these degrees,
award a certificate of completion. According to a 2003 study conducted by the American Academy of Physician Assistants, nearly
49 percent of new graduates received a master's degree from a PA
school. Programs are offered in colleges and universities, teaching
hospitals, and the military, with a prerequisite involving two years
of college (undergraduate) work and prior health care experience.
A few programs run three to four years with prerequisites built into
the curriculum. The majority of students entering PA programs
already have a bachelor of arts or sciences degree and forty-five
months of health care experience before they are admitted to the
PA program.

Subject content in the PA program includes classroom instruction, lab sessions, and clinical rotations (usually in the second year).
In the first year, students concentrate on classes and lab work in the
basic sciences and preclinical subjects. Courses most often taught
include anatomy, physiology, microbiology, pharmacology, patho-
physiology, physical diagnosis, and behavior science.

Following the first nine to fifteen months of training, students
participate in clinical clerkships and preceptorships (a kind of
apprenticeship program in which you learn from the supervising

physician) in various settings such as teaching and community hospitals, clinics, long-term nursing homes, and doctors' offices. Clinical rotations most frequently are offered in obstetrics/gynecology, internal medicine, pediatrics, surgery, family medicine, psychiatry, emergency medicine, and geriatrics. It is an intensive program often involving six days of class and lab work, plus additional hours of study at home or at the library, and little if any time off for holidays or vacations.

Gaining admission to PA schools is no snap either. Many programs receive several applications for each spot. It is therefore in your interest to apply to several schools in which you may be interested to better your chances of being accepted. The average size of graduating classes is between twenty-five to thirty-five people; approximately 4,400 people graduated in 2003. A complete list of accredited schools can be found on the Accreditation Review Commission on the Education for the Physician Assistant website at arc-pa.org. Or you can always research schools through your career resource center or local library.

Admission requirements vary, but studies show that more than half of all applicants have a bachelor's degree. As noted above, college degrees are not required in most programs, but they do help in gaining admission. Many programs require that you have completed courses in biology, English, humanities/social sciences, chemistry, college math, and psychology.

Since school costs vary, write directly to any schools in which you are interested for information on tuition, scholarships, and other financial aid available, as well as information on prerequisites and the admission procedures. Almost always, financial assistance in the form of federal, state, and private loans, as well as scholarships and private grants, is available.

As for almost any area of interest, there are student organizations you can turn to for more information about getting into and excelling in PA school. Many are organizations that are affiliated with an educational program, but some are large, national operations. One such organization is the Student Academy of the American Academy of Physician Assistants (http://saaapa.aapa.org). Student organizations are a valuable source of information and you should take advantage of them.

Surgical Physician Assistant

Physician assistants are found in all areas of medicine, but the majority, more than 50 percent of PAs, work primarily in the area of general or family practice medicine. The next largest concentration of PAs (19 percent) is found in surgery or surgical subspecialties. For each area of specialty, there are professional and student organizations and associations you can contact for more information. (See the Appendix for a list.)

What Surgical PAs Do

As mentioned above, all PAs must work under the supervision of the physician, in this case, the surgeon. When a physician assistant and surgeon begin practicing together, it is vital that they discuss their professional relationship. Usually teamwork and communication are fostered by establishing a broad practice agreement for the team and a job description for the PA that allows the PA to exercise his or her clinical judgment while consulting the supervising surgeon as necessary.

In a typical approach to surgical care with a surgeon as head of the team, the PA might meet the patient in the office or at the hospital, perform the preoperative history and physical, order and compile any necessary tests, and order any necessary preoperative medication or preparations. Prior to surgery, the surgeon reviews the chart and tests and talks to the patient, answering any last-minute questions. PAs frequently serve as first or second assistants in surgery.

Postoperatively, PAs may dictate the operative report, write the postoperative orders as delegated to do so by the surgeon, and manage the surgical patient in the intensive care unit or on the ward. PAs may insert and remove lines and monitoring devices, insert and remove drains, provide the patient with antibiotics and painkillers, remove temporary devices such as pacemakers, and perform other functions traditionally performed by surgeons.

Following the patient's discharge, the surgical PA may continue to follow the patient in another facility or in the office, answer questions from patients and their families, and order prescription refills.

For PAs in orthopedics, common responsibilities include taking evening and weekend calls, providing emergency room coverage, performing admission histories and physicals, caring for simple fractures, assisting in the operating room, conducting postsurgery rounds, ordering x-rays, suturing lacerations, providing patients with preoperative information and postoperative instructions, and performing minor surgical procedures.

Training and Education

Currently there are 131 accredited programs for PAs, of which three offer training for those interested in specializing as surgical physician assistants. These are the University of Alabama at Birmingham (uab.edu), the Weill Medical College at Cornell University (med.cornell.edu), and Cuyahoga Community College (tri-c.cc.oh.us). The educational prerequisites and the length of schooling for surgical PAs is the same as for general PAs. After approximately one year of basic science and medical science classroom work, PA students complete, on average, two thousand hours of supervised clinical practice before graduation. This includes classroom instruction and clinical rotations in medical and surgical specialties. The rotations include family medicine, internal medicine, general surgery, surgical subspecialties, obstetrics and gynecology, pediatrics, emergency medicine, geriatrics, and psychiatry.

Training programs, which average about two years in length, closely resemble those of the PA for the first year. The emphasis is on the basic sciences: microbiology, pharmacology, anatomy, and physiology. Second-year skills, however, both clinical and lecture, emphasize development of surgical skills, pre- and postoperative evaluation, and management of the patient treatment plan.

Licensing and Certification

To ensure that graduating students meet minimum standards of practice and proficiency for all types of PAs, they are required to pass a national examination (the Physician Assistant National Certifying Examination, or PANCE) for certification given annually all over the country. Currently all states require that students be certified by the National Commission on Certification of Physician Assistants (NCCPA), and such certification is a prerequisite to being licensed. To be certified one must be a graduate of an accredited PA program and pass PANCE. Once a PA is certified, he or she must complete a continuous six-year cycle to keep the certificate current. Every two years, a PA must earn and log 100 clinical hours and re-register the certificate with the NCCPA. The Bureau of Labor Statistics predicts that in 2010 there will be nearly 85,000 people in the United States eligible to practice as PAs.

Earnings

What PAs earn depends on several factors: the kind of practice they work for (PAs who work for surgeons, for example, will make more than PAs who work for family practitioners), geographical location, experience, and educational background.

In 2003, the average mean national income for PAs who worked at least thirty-two hours a week was just over $76,000 per year. The comparable mean for PAs who have been in clinical practice for less than one year is $64,565. PAs working in a hospital or medical office earned slightly more than those working in a clinic.

In addition to direct monetary compensation, PAs can receive additional perks in the form of fringe benefits. Some employers pay for mandatory continuing education, which can add up to a couple of thousand dollars a year. Most employers offer a set number of paid days off for vacation, sick time, and education. In addition, the most commonly offered fringe benefit is payment of the PA's liability or malpractice insurance (more on that below).

Job Outlook

The employment outlook for PAs is excellent for the immediate future. In recent years, the demand for health care services has shifted from inpatient surgery to outpatient surgery, and hospital stays have been considerably shortened. Also, because of the downsizing of many corporation staffs, many individuals are foregoing or postponing hospital treatment or surgery for as long as possible.

The federal government has foreseen increasing shortages of PA workers for the next twenty years. The U.S. Department of Labor lists the PA career among its top fifteen career choices and anticipates a 49 percent increase in the number of PA jobs by the year 2012. With the right credentials and certification, PAs should have no trouble finding positions in a wide range of health care facilities. Since PA graduates can be hired at a fraction of the cost of recent M.D. graduates, it seems safe to conclude that the number of PAs will continue to rise in the near future. Then, too, the government continues to relax restrictions on the use of PAs. For example, Medicare now allows physicians to bill the government for services provided by PAs in all settings.

Benefits for both PAs and surgical PAs are good. If you are employed in a private clinic or a government facility or in a hospital or a short-term facility, you will most likely enjoy such attractive benefits as paid vacations, holidays, and sick days as well as participation in pension and investment programs. You also will qualify for health care coverage for yourself and your family.

Legal Considerations

These days, with the incidence of malpractice suits a very real consideration in the practice of medicine, should you as a PA be concerned? The answer is a qualified yes, since both the physician and the PA who works in his or her office share in their liability in such malpractice suits. However, since this is the case, it is highly unlikely that your physician employer would authorize you to do work beyond your capability and experience. It should be further noted that studies have shown that when PAs are employed, patients on the whole are highly pleased because waiting periods are reduced, they receive more attention, and doctor-patient relationships are improved, which tends to reduce the risk of malpractice suits.

Physicians must notify their malpractice insurance carrier when they hire a physician assistant. The PA is added to the physician's insurance, which increases the premium by a few hundred dollars. The physician's existing policy limits stay in place, even with the extra premium. Additionally, standard practice is for the PA to have an individual policy as well. In fact, the American Academy of Physician Assistants tells its members: "Don't settle for being insured under your employer's policy. Insist on your own personal policy." A PA working in a primary care practice can generally buy a $100,000 to $300,000 policy for less than $600 a year. But, of course, rates and coverage limits are greater for PAs working in higher-risk areas, such as obstetrics, surgery, and cardiac catheterization labs. Many physicians offer to purchase the PA's policy as a recruiting incentive or fringe benefit, although it certainly isn't required. No matter who pays for the policy, it belongs to the PA, and the physician's liability remains the same.

Malpractice insurance policies for PAs entitle them to their own defense attorney and protect them if they change jobs or if the employing physician closes his or her practice before a malpractice claim is filed. It also reimburses the PA for time away from work to give depositions, pays for legal fees to defend a professional license before a state agency, and offers access to the insurer's risk-management consultants. A separate insurance policy would also cover the PA for any damages he or she must pay, whether to a patient or to compensate an employer.

Pathologist Assistant

The pathologist assistant profession began as a training program at the Veterans Administration Medical Center at Duke University in 1969. Additional programs were established in Veterans Administration Medical Centers in Alabama and Connecticut a short time later. These baccalaureate degree programs were the first to formally train men and women to assume responsibility for functions originally performed by anatomic pathologists and other personnel studying disease processes in the human body.

The pathologist assistant is an allied health professional who is qualified by academic and practical training to assist in providing service in anatomic pathology under the direction and supervision of a pathologist, who specializes in the study, analysis, and diagnosis of changes caused by diseases of the tissue and the blood. Pathologist assistants participate in the examination, dissection, and processing of tissues and in gross autopsy dissection.

Pathologist assistants are employed in a variety of settings, including community and regional hospitals, university medical centers, private pathology laboratories, and medical examiner offices. The ability to relate to people, a capacity for calm and reasoned judgment, and a demonstration of commitment to patient quality care are essential to excel in this job. The high degree of responsibility assumed by the pathologist assistant requires skills and abilities necessary to provide those services appropriate for an anatomic pathology setting.

What Pathologist Assistants Do

Although the pathologist assistant profession has been in existence since the late 1960s, the exact definition of the job duties performed by the pathologist assistant role will often vary across settings. This is most likely due to the relatively small number of people working in the field, the variability in training and education, and the lack of a nationally required examination to achieve licensure for employment.

Depending on the pathologist for whom a pathologist assistant works, the following are a few of the tasks that one might be required to perform:

- Assist in autopsies, including external examination, on-site
  organ inspections, evisceration or removal of internal organs,
  and dissection of organs and tissue
- Obtain biological specimens for analysis (blood cultures,
  viral cultures, toxicological material, and so on)
- Dictate or record data on your findings
- Assist the pathologist in preparation of preliminary diagnoses
  and summarize the clinical history of same
- Provide gross description and complete dissection of surgical
  specimens
- Select and submit tissue sections for microscopic analysis
  (that is, frozen and permanent sections for light, electron,
  and fluorescent microscopy) for both postmortem
  examinations and for examination of human surgical
  specimens

Working with diseased tissue of the dead does require a certain
amount of dedication and fortitude. If you think you would be
uncomfortable in dissecting corpses or handling diseased tissue,
you might do well to consider some other paramedical career.

Training and Education

Some pathologist assistants receive their training on the job from a
practicing pathologist. More and more often, however, those interested in the field are turning to higher education, which tends to
yield greater job opportunities and better pay. There are five schools
accredited by the National Accrediting Agency for Clinical Laboratory Sciences. These schools offer training programs for pathologist assistants; four of these schools offer master's programs.
Programs vary in length and in the degree awarded, but they usu-

ally result in a bachelor of science or a master of health science. Most pathologist assistant programs run two years in length—one year of academic work and a year of clinical training.

Following are the five schools accredited by the National Accrediting Agency for Clinical Laboratory Sciences:

Duke University
Department of Pathology
P.O. Box 3712
Durham, North Carolina 27710
http://biosci.mc.duke.edu
(Master of Health Science, two-year program)

Ohio State University
N-308A Doan Hall
410 West Tenth Avenue
Columbus, Ohio 43210
pathology.med.ohio-state.edu
(Master of Science, two-year program)

Quinnipiac University
275 Mount Carmel Avenue
Hamden, Connecticut 06518
quinnipiac.edu
(Master of Health Science, two-year program)

University of Maryland
Department of Pathology
22 South Greene Street
Baltimore, Maryland 21201
vprgs.umd.edu
(Master of Science, two-year program)

Wayne State University
Department of Mortuary Sciences
5439 Woodward Avenue
Detroit, Michigan 48202
med.wayne.edu/pathology/anatomicpathologyassistantsprogram.htm
(Bachelor of Science, two-year program)

Licensing and Certification

At present there is no national certification or licensing examination for pathologist assistants. The American Association of Pathologists Assistants (AAPA), the only national professional organization for pathologist assistants, administers a competency exam to its 750 members, but this is completely voluntary. A pathologist assistant need not pass this exam to work in this area. Over the past decade, the AAPA has been working to establish training standards for pathologist assistants with national certification as the ultimate goal. Currently, the National Commission on Certification is drafting recommendations concerning training and professional standards, which will ultimately lead to a national certification examination. Today, however, only a few states require that a pathologist assistant be licensed to work in that state.

Earnings

As a beginner, in some parts of the country, a starting salary for a pathologist assistant may be as high as $55,000 a year; with experience and a master's degree, salaries can reach $75,000 a year. Additional benefits include health care and retirement benefits, continuing medical education funding, professional association dues payment, and travel monies.

Job Outlook

Although the occupation is smaller than that of the physician assistant, the demand for qualified pathologist assistants is growing every year. Increasing pressures on health care systems to control costs have led to an increasing reliance on allied health personnel and physician extenders in general, and for pathology laboratories, in particular. Demand for pathologist assistants is high, and the employer demand exceeds the supply of new graduates in the field. Openings for pathologist assistants exist in all areas of the United States. Most positions currently are in community hospitals, providing a combination of autopsy and surgical pathology services. Positions in teaching hospitals, research environments, and private laboratories are also usually available.

5

OTHER PARAPROFESSIONALS IN THE MEDICAL FIELD

WHILE THE ALLIED health paraprofessional careers described in this chapter are jobs that require less training and education than those in the previous chapter, they are no less important. These jobs help medical offices and institutions run smoothly and efficiently, and these positions are often held by the first person worried patients meet before they see the doctor. The jobs in this chapter offer the flexibility of a wide range of working environments and required skill sets, but primarily they require that the paraprofessional possess a combination of clinical and administrative expertise. The best part of all, these jobs are in incredible demand in all areas of the country, and the job growth for these positions shows no signs of slowing!

Medical Assistant

It would be quite simple to take the terms "medical assistant" and "physician assistant" to mean the same thing, but don't get the two confused. To be sure, they both offer substantial support to the physician, but there is a world of difference between them. PAs serve as physician extenders, as noted in Chapter 4. They enable the physician to serve more patients than would otherwise be possible. They interview, examine, and treat patients under the direction of a physician and are, in effect, practicing medicine, even though they are not doing so independently.

Medical assistants, on the other hand, provide invaluable support to physicians through their skills and services and they also serve as clerks or administrators in doctors' offices. In effect, they are the intermediary between doctors and patients and they keep doctors' offices running smoothly. This is why nearly all physicians in practice today have at least one skilled medical assistant in the office. To put it simply, the medical assistant is the link between the doctor and the patient and between the doctor and professional colleagues and suppliers of medications and equipment.

Medical assistants held about 365,000 jobs in 2002, making this by far the largest of the allied health paraprofessional careers. Almost 60 percent worked in the offices of physicians; about 14 percent worked in public and private hospitals, including inpatient and outpatient facilities; and almost 10 percent worked in offices of other health practitioners, such as chiropractors and podiatrists. The rest worked mostly in outpatient care centers, public and private educational services, other ambulatory health care services, state and local government agencies, medical and diagnostic laboratories, nursing care facilities, and employment services. Most full-time medical assistants work a regular forty-hour week, although some work part-time, evenings, or weekends.

What Medical Assistants Do

Medical assistants shoulder the burden of running the office so that physicians can concentrate on diagnosing and treating patients. Specific duties vary from office to office, depending on the size and location of the office and the physician's specialty, and according to state law for the clinical duties a medical assistant can perform. In small practices, medical assistants usually are "generalists," handling both administrative and clinical duties and reporting directly to an office manager, physician, or other health practitioner. Those in large practices tend to specialize in a particular area, under the supervision of department administrators. The backbone of the job as a medical assistant may include any of the following clinical or patient-oriented duties:

- Taking medical histories
- Preparing patients for examination and assisting as the doctor examines them
- Recording vital signs—pulse, blood pressure, temperature, and so forth
- Sterilizing medical equipment and instruments
- Disposing of contaminated supplies
- Collecting and preparing laboratory specimens and performing basic laboratory tests on blood and urine in the physician's office
- Preparing and administering medications as directed by the doctor
- Instructing patients on medication usage and diet
- Authorizing drug refills as directed by the doctor
- Handling such procedures as drawing blood, taking EKGs, removing stitches, changing dressings, and preparing patients for x-rays

In addition to these duties, which are more medical in nature, the medical assistant may be responsible for clerical and administrative duties, including arranging examining rooms and equipment, purchasing and maintaining supplies, keeping the premises clean, answering phone calls and receiving patients, scheduling appointments, updating and filling out insurance forms and records, handling billing and bookkeeping, and arranging for hospital admissions, lab services, or other medical treatments.

Training and Education

Because the operation and handling of medical care is complex and the job requirements are demanding, few doctors are able to provide on-the-job training for their staffs. Today's medical assistants receive their training at one of several hundred programs located all over the country that are accredited by one of the two accrediting agencies: the Commission on Accreditation of Allied Health Education Programs (CAAHEP), which accredits nearly five hundred programs, and the Accrediting Bureau of Health Education Schools (ABHES), which accredits an additional two hundred programs. For a complete list of the schools accredited by these organizations, visit their websites (see the Appendix).

Most employers prefer graduates of formal programs in medical assisting. Such programs are offered in vocational-technical high schools, postsecondary vocational schools, and community and junior colleges. Postsecondary programs usually last either one year, resulting in a certificate or diploma, or two years, resulting in an associate degree. Courses cover anatomy, physiology, and medical terminology, as well as typing, transcription, recordkeeping, accounting, and insurance processing. Students learn laboratory techniques, clinical and diagnostic procedures, pharmaceutical principles, the administration of medications, and first aid. They study office practices, patient relations, medical law, and ethics. Accredited programs include an internship that provides practical experience in physicians' offices, hospitals, or other health care facilities. An externship in a physician's office is required to provide practical experience.

Formal training in medical assisting, while generally preferred, is not always required. Some medical assistants are trained on the job, although this practice is less common than in the past. Applicants usually need a high school diploma or the equivalent. Recommended high school courses include mathematics, health, biology, typing, bookkeeping, computers, and office skills. Volunteer experience in the health care field also is helpful.

Licensing and Certification

Although medical assistants are not licensed, some states require them to take a test or a course before they can perform certain tasks, such as taking x-rays. Employers prefer to hire experienced workers or certified applicants who have passed a national examination, indicating that the medical assistant meets certain standards of competence. Certification, which is highly desirable in landing a job and advancing in this career, is available after graduation from an accredited program. Certification indicates your performance is up to national standards, which physicians increasingly are looking for in hiring medical assistants. Examinations are offered by either the American Association of Medical Assistants (AAMA) or the American Medical Technologists (AMT). The AAMA awards the Certified Medical Assistant designation, while the AMT awards the Registered Medical Assistant certification. The AAMA certification exam is given annually in January and June at more than two hundred test centers throughout the United States. The AMT exam is given throughout the year at various testing centers in the United States.

Earnings

Salaries for medical assistants, as is true of virtually all paraprofessional careers, depend on local salary scales, the employee's background and experience, and the workplace, as well as specific job responsibilities. For instance, a recent AAMA survey showed that primarily administrative medical assistants earn more than those whose duties are primarily clinical. As you would expect, average salary increases with experience.

The earnings of medical assistants vary, depending on their experience, skill level, and location. Median annual earnings of medical assistants were $23,940 in 2002. The middle 50 percent earned between $20,260 and $28,410. The lowest 10 percent earned less than $17,640, and the highest 10 percent earned more than $34,130. Median annual earnings in the industries employing the largest numbers of medical assistants in 2002 were as follows:

General medical and surgical hospitals	$24,460
Offices of physicians	$24,260
Outpatient care centers	$23,980
Other ambulatory health care services	$23,440
Offices of other health practitioners	$21,620

Keep in mind that these average salaries apply to all forms of medical assistants, including the podiatric and ophthalmic medical assistant. Location also affects salaries, with the highest earnings reported in the New England, middle Atlantic, and Pacific states, and the lowest in the east and west north-central states and the east and west south-central states.

Job Outlook

According to the Bureau of Labor Statistics, the increasing use of medical assistants in the rapidly growing health care industries will result in fast employment growth for the occupation through the year 2012. In fact, the medical assistant is projected to be the fastest-growing occupation in terms of numbers employed over the 2002–12 period. This is due to several factors: the expansion in health care jobs due to the increased medical needs of an aging population, increases in the number of physicians, more diagnostic and test procedures, and finally, more paperwork. Most job openings, however, will result from the need to replace those who have left the profession, died, or retired. Employment growth will be driven by the increase in the number of group practices, clinics, and other health care facilities that need a high proportion of support personnel, particularly the flexible medical assistant who can handle both administrative and clinical duties. Medical assistants work primarily in outpatient settings, which are expected to exhibit much faster-than-average growth. In view of the preference of many health care employers for trained personnel, job prospects should be best for medical assistants with formal training or experience, and particularly for those with certification.

Medical assistants may be able to advance to office manager. They may qualify for a variety of administrative support occupations or may teach medical assisting. With additional education, some enter other health occupations, such as nursing and medical technology.

Podiatric Assistant

Americans, as a whole, spend a great deal of time on their feet. As our older population becomes more active across all age groups, the need for foot care will become increasingly important to maintaining a healthy lifestyle.

The human foot is a complex structure. It contains 26 bones—plus muscles, nerves, ligaments, and blood vessels—and is designed for balance and mobility. The 52 bones in your feet make up about one-fourth of all the bones in your body. Podiatrists, also known as doctors of podiatric medicine (D.P.M.s), diagnose and treat disorders, diseases, and injuries of the foot and lower leg to keep this part of the body working properly. To become a podiatrist, you must successfully complete a four-year training program leading to a D.P.M. In addition, you must pass a state-licensing exam to practice in any state.

Podiatrists treat corns, calluses, ingrown toenails, bunions, heel spurs, and arch problems; ankle and foot injuries, deformities, and infections; and foot complaints associated with diseases such as diabetes. To treat these problems, podiatrists prescribe drugs, order physical therapy, set fractures, and perform surgery. They also fit corrective inserts called orthotics, design plaster casts to correct deformities, and design custom-made shoes. Podiatrists may use a force plate to help design these corrective devices. Patients walk across a plate connected to a computer that "reads" their feet, picking up pressure points and weight distribution. From the computer readout, podiatrists order the correct design or recommend another kind of treatment.

The foot may be the first area to show signs of serious conditions such as arthritis, diabetes, and heart disease. For example, diabetics are prone to foot ulcers and infections due to poor circulation.

Podiatrists consult with and refer patients to other health practitioners when they detect symptoms of these disorders.

What Podiatric Assistants Do

The podiatric assistant helps the podiatrist provide care for a wide range of patients. The podiatric assistant, as is the case of all allied health paraprofessionals, is qualified by schooling and clinical experience to serve patients under the direction of a licensed podiatrist. Duties of the podiatric assistant will depend largely on experience and training, the kind of podiatric practice in which he or she works, the volume of patients seen, and the number of additional assistants employed. The following list describes the common duties the podiatric assistant might perform:

- Preparing patients for treatment, including padding and strapping
- Taking and recording patient histories
- Applying surgical dressings
- Preparing and sterilizing instruments and equipment
- Providing postoperative instructions to the patient
- Exposing and developing x-rays
- Assisting in biomedical evaluation and negative castings
- Handling routine office procedures, including answering the telephone, scheduling appointments, and maintaining inventory

Podiatric assistants typically work in a podiatrist's office, which is usually not in a hospital. They also may spend time visiting patients in nursing homes, but they normally have fewer after-hours emergencies than other doctors have. Podiatrists with private practices set their own hours but may work evenings and weekends to meet the needs of their patients.

Training and Education

While some podiatric assistants receive their training on the job, most employers prefer graduates of formal programs in medical assisting. Such programs are offered in vocational-technical high schools, postsecondary vocational schools, community and junior colleges, and in colleges and universities.

Postsecondary programs usually last either one year, resulting in a certificate or diploma, or two years, resulting in an associate degree. Courses cover anatomy, physiology, and medical terminology as well as typing, transcription, recordkeeping, accounting, and insurance processing. Students learn laboratory techniques, clinical and diagnostic procedures, pharmaceutical principles, medication administration, and first aid. They study office practices, patient relations, medical law, and ethics. Accredited programs often include an internship that provides practical experience in physicians' offices, hospitals, or other health care facilities.

Licensing and Certification

While there are no national licensing requirements for podiatric assistants, some states require licenses to practice various procedures. In this case, the procedure most frequently performed that may require additional licensing and education is the x-ray.

To gain employment, podiatric assistants must typically be a high school graduate or equivalent and complete an approved program or course of study in theoretical consideration underlying radiation hygiene and podiatric radiological practices through a vocational or technical school or a community college. Some states require that students complete a radiographic clinical program sufficient to demonstrate proficiency to a podiatric sponsor with at least fifty total exposures with direct supervision from a podiatrist or certified person to take podiatric x-rays. The program or course of study may include approximately twenty working days of clinical training in a podiatric office or clinic. A podiatry assistant who holds a permit to practice limited diagnostic radiography in the extremities or the foot by the Bureau of Environmental Health may apply for and be granted a certificate in podiatric radiography without meeting a particular state's training or examination requirements.

Some podiatric assistants decide to work toward certification and the designation PMAC (Podiatric Medical Assistant, Certified) from the American Society of Podiatric Medical Assistants. To qualify, the podiatric assistant must be a member of the society, have worked in a podiatry office for a minimum of one year, and pass a written exam given by the society. In addition, he or she must complete a number of continuing education courses every year to retain certification. The purpose of this certification is to elevate the prestige and professionalism of the work of the podiatric assistant.

Earnings

Earnings for podiatric assistants are comparable to that of medical assistants (see above).

Job Outlook

Job prospects for podiatric assistants should remain good for many years. Most podiatrists currently employ at least two assistants, and that number is expected to rise. As our population ages, the demand for treatment of foot problems should rise, and podiatrists will rely increasingly on podiatric assistants to handle routine measurements.

6

PARAPROFESSIONALS IN EMERGENCY MEDICAL SERVICES

EVERY DAY IN communities large and small across the United States, frantic calls come in on the emergency 911 network or to hospitals or emergency centers for help to persons who have experienced life-or-death injuries involving automobile accidents, heart attacks, strokes, poisonings, accidental electrocution, near drowning, gunshot wounds, and many other situations requiring immediate medical attention. Usually the first ones on the scene are the emergency medical technicians (EMTs) or the paramedics, who are EMTs with advanced training to perform more difficult prehospital medical procedures.

The work of the EMT and paramedic occurs in an emergency setting requiring split-second decisions and fast reflexes. Every day will bring new challenges and rewards. It is a high-energy, fast-paced job, and one that provides a vital service to our communities.

Before we begin the discussion of these emergency medical service providers, it is important to understand a couple of things. First, every state has an EMS lead agency or State Office of Emergency Medical Services, and many of these offices have websites that provide information to the public. If you are interested in learning more, you should look up your state's agency online through a keyword search. In addition, it is important to know that EMS is a local service and, therefore, differs in capability, service provider, and in a variety of other ways across the nation. The descriptions in this chapter are a good overview of what these jobs entail, but you should contact your state EMS office for more precise information.

Emergency Medical Technicians and Paramedics

Working under the instructions of medical officers at a central office, EMTs and paramedics work in teams of two and drive specially equipped emergency vehicles (ambulances) to the scene of the emergency. They may work for the police or fire departments, for hospitals, or for private ambulance services or rescue squads. Arriving on the scene, they render first aid or cardiopulmonary resuscitation (CPR) to victims of heart attacks, strokes, and other medical emergencies. If necessary, they may request additional help on the scene from police, fire, or electric company workers, or they may seek volunteer help from bystanders in directing traffic or removing obstacles.

EMTs and paramedics must do a bit of detective work as they try to find out the nature and seriousness of the patient's injuries or illness or if he or she has any preexisting conditions such as heart problems, epilepsy, or diabetes that could affect his or her condition. Following strict guidelines for the procedures they perform, they provide prescribed medical treatment.

EMTs and paramedics use special equipment, such as backboards, to immobilize patients before placing them on stretchers and securing them in the ambulance for transport to a medical facility. Usually, one EMT or paramedic drives while the other monitors the patient's vital signs and gives additional care as needed. Some EMTs work as part of the flight crew of helicopters that transport critically ill or injured patients to hospital trauma centers.

At the medical facility, EMTs and paramedics help transfer patients to the emergency department, report their observations and actions to emergency room staff, and may provide additional emergency treatment. After each run, EMTs and paramedics replace used supplies and check equipment. If a transported patient had a contagious disease, the EMTs and paramedics must decontaminate the interior of the ambulance and report certain cases to the proper authorities.

EMTs and paramedics held about 179,000 jobs in 2002. Most career EMTs and paramedics work in metropolitan areas, whereas volunteers provide the services of EMTs and paramedics in smaller cities, towns, and rural areas. These individuals volunteer for fire departments, emergency medical services (EMS), or hospitals, and may respond to only a few calls for service per month or may answer the majority of calls, especially in smaller communities. EMTs and paramedics work closely with firefighters, who often are certified to act as first responders.

Full-time and part-time paid EMTs and paramedics are employed in a number of industries. According to the Bureau of Labor statistics, about four out of ten worked as employees of private ambulance services; three out of ten worked in local government for fire departments, public ambulance services, and EMS; and another two out of ten were found in hospitals, working full-time within the medical facility or responding to calls in ambulances or helicopters to transport critically ill or injured patients. The remainder worked in various industries providing emergency services.

What EMTs and Paramedics Do

There are several levels of EMTs; what kind of medical treatment EMTs are legally allowed to provide depends largely upon which category they fall into. To determine this, the National Registry of Emergency Medical Technicians (NREMT) registers emergency medical service providers at four levels: First Responder, EMT-Basic, EMT-Intermediate, and EMT-Paramedic. Some states, however, do their own certification and use numeric ratings from one to four to distinguish levels of proficiency.

The lowest-level workers, the First Responders, are trained to provide basic emergency medical care to stabilize the injured persons because they tend to be the first persons to arrive at the scene of an incident. Many firefighters, police officers, and other emergency workers have this level of training. A First Responder is not an EMT; it is simply a certification of training that a person working in emergency services has obtained.

The EMT-Basic, also known as EMT-1, represents the first component of the emergency medical technician system. An EMT-1 is trained to care for patients at the scene of an accident and while transporting patients by ambulance to the hospital under medical direction. The EMT-1 has the emergency skills to assess a patient's condition and manage respiratory, cardiac, and trauma emergencies. Those who have attained the EMT-1 certification can handle the following procedures after having fully assessed the patient and determined the extent of injuries and kinds of treatment called for:

- Treating for shock, administering oxygen or CPR
- Immobilizing fractures, bandaging wounds
- Opening airways, restoring breathing, controlling bleeding
- Rendering first-aid treatment to heart attack or accident victims, disturbed patients, or poison or burn victims
- Using a defibrillator to give lifesaving shocks to patients whose heartbeat may be faint or may have stopped altogether

EMT-Intermediates, also known as EMT-2 and EMT-3, have more advanced training and can handle such additional procedures as the administration of intravenous fluids, the use of manual defibrillators to give lifesaving shocks to a stopped heart, and the application of advanced airway techniques and equipment to assist patients experiencing respiratory emergencies.

Those in the last category of EMTs—EMT-Paramedics—have had the most extensive training. These paramedics are trained to treat patients with minor injuries on the scene of an accident or at their home without transporting them to a medical facility. Emergency treatment for more complicated problems is carried out under the direction of medical doctors by radio preceding or during transport. In addition to the actions listed above, EMT-Paramedics are qualified to handle procedures such as:

- Administering drugs by mouth or intravenously
- Interpreting and reading electrocardiograms (EKGs)
- Performing endotracheal intubation
- Using monitors and other complex equipment

Because emergencies can happen at any time, day or night and on weekends, EMTs and paramedics may be called in to work odd shifts and in harsh weather. In addition, they may have to work the midnight shift, weekends, and holidays. EMTs and paramedics work both indoors and outdoors, in all types of weather. They are required to do considerable kneeling, bending, and heavy lifting. These workers risk noise-induced hearing loss from sirens and back injuries from lifting patients. In addition, EMTs and paramedics may be exposed to diseases such as hepatitis-B and AIDS, as well as violence from drug overdose victims or mentally unstable patients. The work is not only physically strenuous, but also stressful, involving life-or-death situations and suffering patients. Nonetheless, many people find the work exciting and challenging and enjoy the opportunity to help others.

Training and Education

Formal training is needed to become an EMT or paramedic. Training is offered at progressive levels, as described above: EMT-Basic (EMT-1), EMT-Intermediate (EMT-2 and EMT-3), and EMT-Paramedic (EMT-4). EMT-Basic coursework typically emphasizes emergency skills, such as managing respiratory, trauma, and cardiac emergencies, and patient assessment. Formal courses are often combined with time in an emergency room or ambulance. The program also provides instruction and practice in dealing with bleeding, fractures, airway obstruction, cardiac arrest, and emergency childbirth. Students learn how to use and maintain common emergency equipment, such as backboards, suction devices, splints, oxygen delivery systems, and stretchers. Graduates of approved EMT-Basic training programs who pass a written and practical examination administered by the state certifying agency or the NREMT earn the title "Registered EMT-Basic." The EMT-Basic course also is a prerequisite for EMT-Intermediate and EMT-Paramedic training.

EMT-Intermediate training requirements vary from state to state. Applicants can opt to receive training in EMT-Shock Trauma, wherein the caregiver learns to start intravenous fluids and give certain medications, or in EMT-Cardiac, which includes learning heart rhythms and administering advanced medications. Training commonly includes thirty-five to fifty-five hours of additional instruction beyond EMT-Basic coursework and covers patient assessment as well as the use of advanced airway devices and intravenous fluids. Prerequisites for taking the EMT-Intermediate examination include registration as an EMT-Basic, required classroom work, and a specified amount of clinical experience.

The most advanced level of training for this occupation is EMT-Paramedic. At this level, the caregiver receives additional training in body function and learns more advanced skills. The technology program usually lasts up to two years and results in an associate degree in applied science. Such education prepares the graduate to take the NREMT examination and become certified as an EMT-Paramedic. Extensive related coursework and clinical and field experience are required. Due to the longer training requirement, almost all EMT-Paramedics are in paid positions rather than in volunteer positions. Refresher courses and continuing education are available for EMTs and paramedics at all levels.

EMTs and paramedics should be emotionally stable; have good dexterity, agility, and physical coordination; and be able to lift and carry heavy loads. They also need good eyesight (corrective lenses may be used) with accurate color vision.

Advancement beyond the EMT-Paramedic level usually means leaving fieldwork. An EMT-Paramedic can become a supervisor, operations manager, administrative director, or executive director of emergency services. Some EMTs and paramedics become instructors, dispatchers, or physician assistants, while others move into sales or marketing of emergency medical equipment. A number of people become EMTs and paramedics to assess their interest in health care and then decide to return to school and become registered nurses, physicians, or other health workers.

Licensing and Certification

To earn the registered EMT-Basic designation, the EMT must have completed an approved EMT-Basic course and pass a written and practical examination given by the state regulatory agency or the National Registry of Emergency Medical Technicians. Beyond this, you must have completed the additional class work, clinical experience, and internship required to take the EMT-Intermediate exam offered either by your state regulatory agency or the NREMT. To take the examination of EMT-Paramedic designation, you must also have completed the EMT-Paramedic training program and have passed a written and practical examination.

All fifty states have a certification procedure. In most states and the District of Columbia, registration with the NREMT is required at some or all levels of certification. Other states administer their own certification examination or provide the option of taking the NREMT examination. Once the EMT has achieved certification, he or she must maintain it. To do so, he or she must reregister, usually every two years. During the period between recertification, the EMT must be working as an EMT and be able to meet a continuing education requirement.

Earnings

Earnings of EMTs and paramedics depend on the employment set-ting and geographic location as well as the individual's training and experience. According to the Bureau of Labor Statistics, median annual earnings of EMTs and paramedics were $24,030 in 2002. The middle 50 percent earned between $19,040 and $31,600. The lowest 10 percent earned less than $15,530, and the highest 10 per-cent earned more than $41,980. Median annual earnings in the industries employing the largest numbers of EMTs and paramedics in 2002 were:

Local government	$27,440
General medical and surgical hospitals	$24,760
Other ambulatory health care services	$22,180

Those in emergency medical services who are part of fire or police departments receive the same benefits as firefighters or police offi-cers. For example, many are covered by pension plans that provide retirement at half pay after twenty or twenty-five years of service or if the worker is disabled in the line of duty.

Job Outlook

Opportunities for EMTs will vary somewhat depending upon where they are employed. Currently, there are more than eight hun-dred thousand EMTs and paramedics providing emergency med-ical services to the citizens of the United States. Overall, according to the Bureau of Labor Statistics, employment of emergency med-ical technicians and paramedics is expected to grow faster than the average for all occupations through 2012. Competition will be especially keen in police, fire, and rescue units because these areas tend to pay the most and offer the best benefits. Conversely, job openings in hospitals and private ambulance services will not be so competitive since they pay less and offer less attractive benefits. Aside from that, the same forces that serve to spur the entire array of paraprofessional careers will be at work here: the aging and expansion of the population with accompanying need for more medical treatment. Also expected to generate more jobs is the fact that even smaller communities are switching from volunteer emergency medical services to paid ones. Job turnover is high, reflecting the stress that EMTs and paramedics work under, the limited chances for advancement, and the relatively modest pay scales, especially when working for private companies.

7

PARAPROFESSIONALS IN THE NURSING FIELD

THE FIELD OF nursing has many definitions, but the essence of nursing is that nurses combine the art of caring with the science of health care. Unlike medicine, the focus of nursing is not on a particular health problem but on the whole patient and his or her response to treatment. Care of the patient and a firm base of scientific knowledge are indispensable elements of being a good nurse.

Many nurses say they felt "called" to a career in nursing, a field that combines the use of high-tech equipment and cutting-edge science with hands-on care and personal interactions. Nurses can make an incredible difference in the lives of the sick and hurting. Because of this, they must be compassionate, quick-thinking people who are able to communicate well with a range of people of all races, old and young, men and women.

This chapter focuses on those jobs that provide assistance to the registered nurse. Typically, these jobs require little or no additional education beyond high school. You must definitely be a people person to do well in and enjoy this line of work. Many people use the jobs described in this chapter as a stepping-stone to other careers in health care and as a means of assessing whether or not the field of health care, and nursing in particular, is a good fit.

Licensed Practical Nurse

Licensed practical nurses (LPNs) care for the sick, injured, convalescent, and disabled under the direction of physicians, registered nurses, and even dentists. To be effective in their job, LPNs should have a caring, sympathetic nature. They should be emotionally stable, because work with the sick and injured can be stressful. They also should have keen observational, decision-making, and communication skills. As part of a health care team, they must be able to follow orders and work under close supervision.

Most licensed practical nurses in hospitals and nursing care facilities work a forty-hour week, but because patients need around-the-clock care, some work nights, weekends, and holidays. They often stand for long periods and help patients move in bed, stand, or walk, so they must be very careful not to injure themselves. Special—and very expensive—shoes are often worn to help prevent sore feet.

According to the Bureau of Labor Statistics, licensed practical nurses held about 702,000 jobs in 2002. About 28 percent of LPNs worked in hospitals, 26 percent in nursing care facilities, and another 12 percent in offices of physicians. Others worked for home health care services, employment services, community care facilities for the elderly, public and private educational services, outpatient care centers, and federal, state, and local government agencies; about one in five worked part-time.

The work of the LPN can be very stressful, both emotionally and physically. LPNs may face hazards from caustic chemicals, radiation, and infectious diseases such as hepatitis, so they must be fully immunized before they start work. (Usually the employer will take care of this free of charge.) They often must deal with the stress of heavy workloads, and some of the patients they care for may be confused, irrational, agitated, or uncooperative. In general, however, this is a job that can offer a great amount of satisfaction in seeing tangible results from efforts—a clean, comfortable, healing patient.

What LPNs Do

LPNs provide basic bedside care, monitor their patients, and report adverse reactions to medications or treatments. In addition to providing routine bedside care, LPNs in nursing care facilities help evaluate residents' needs, develop care plans, and supervise the care provided by nursing assistants. In doctors' offices and clinics, they also may make appointments, keep records, and perform other clerical duties. LPNs who work in private homes may prepare meals and teach family members simple nursing tasks to help care for their loved ones. To help keep patients comfortable, LPNs assist with bathing, dressing, and personal hygiene. In states where the law allows, they may administer prescribed medicines or start intravenous fluids. Some LPNs help deliver, care for, and feed infants. Experienced LPNs may supervise nursing assistants and other assistants. In addition, LPNs do the following tasks:

- Take vital signs such as temperature, blood pressure, pulse, and respiration
- Prepare and give injections and enemas

- Monitor catheters
- Apply dressings
- Treat bedsores
- Give alcohol rubs and massages
- Collect samples for testing
- Perform routine laboratory tests
- Feed patients and record food and fluid intake and output

Training and Education

A high school diploma or its equivalent usually is required for entry, although some programs accept candidates without a diploma or are designed as part of a high school curriculum.

In 2002, approximately 1,100 state-approved programs provided training in practical nursing. Almost six out of ten students were enrolled in technical or vocational schools, while three out of ten were in community and junior colleges. Others were in high schools, hospitals, and colleges and universities.

Most practical nursing programs last about one year and include both classroom study and supervised clinical practice (patient care). Classroom study covers basic nursing concepts and patient care–related subjects, including anatomy, physiology, medical-surgical nursing, pediatrics, obstetrics, psychiatric nursing, the administration of drugs, nutrition, and first aid. Clinical practice usually is in a hospital, but sometimes includes other settings.

Licensing and Certification

All states and the District of Columbia require LPNs to pass a licensing examination after completing a state-approved practical nursing program. Licensing is different from certification in that licensing defines the legal scope of practice for the LPN and certification shows recognition of accomplishment. An LPN cannot legally work without licensure. View the website for the National Council for State Boards of Nursing for more information at ncsbn.org.

Certification in various areas of specialty is offered by several nursing organizations. The National Association for Practical Nurse Education and Service offers certification in long-term care and pharmacology, and the National Federation of Licensed Practical Nurses awards certification in IV therapy and gerontology. By achieving these certifications, LPNs show their employers that they have mastered practical nurse–level care in these areas.

Earnings

Health insurance benefits are a substantial perk to working as an LPN as out-of-pocket expenses are exorbitant. There is ample opportunity for working overtime in this position, which may substantially add to earnings. In addition, shift premiums increase pay by working afternoons or the overnight shifts.

According to the Bureau of Labor Statistics, median annual earnings of licensed practical nurses were $31,440 in 2002. The middle 50 percent earned between $26,430 and $37,050. The lowest 10 percent earned less than $22,860, and the highest 10 percent earned more than $44,040. Median annual earnings in the industries employing the largest numbers of licensed practical nurses in 2002 were as follows:

Employment services	$40,550
Home health care services	$32,850
Nursing care facilities	$32,220

General medical and surgical hospitals $30,310
Offices of physicians $28,710

Job Outlook

Employment of LPNs is expected to grow about as fast as the average for all occupations through 2012 in response to the long-term care needs of an increasing elderly population and the general growth of health care. Replacement needs will be a major source of job openings, as many workers leave the occupation permanently.

Applicants for jobs in hospitals may face competition as the number of hospital jobs for LPNs declines. An increasing proportion of sophisticated procedures, which once were performed only in hospitals, is being performed in physicians' offices and in outpatient care centers such as ambulatory surgical and emergency medical centers, due largely to advances in technology. Consequently, employment of LPNs is projected to grow faster than average in these sectors as health care expands outside the traditional hospital setting.

Employment of LPNs in nursing care facilities is expected to grow faster than the average. Such facilities will offer the most new jobs for LPNs as the number of aged and disabled persons in need of long-term care rises. In addition to caring for the aged and the disabled, LPNs in nursing care facilities will care for the increasing number of patients who will have been discharged from the hospital, but have not recovered enough to return home.

Employment of LPNs is expected to grow much faster than average in home health care services. This growth is in response to an increasing number of older persons with functional disabilities, consumer preference for care in the home, and technological advances that make it possible to bring increasingly complex treatments into the home. In addition, many patients feel more comfortable in their home environment than in a hospital setting.

Nursing Assistant

Nursing assistants help care for physically ill, injured, disabled, or infirm individuals confined to hospitals and nursing care facilities. They are the backbone of any health care facility and often spend the most time with patients, providing them with much needed human contact. They perform many of the vital functions that keep patients clean and comfortable; all of these are necessary acts to promote patients' mental and physical healing. Even so, this is a low-prestige job within the medical and nursing fields, yet it is an occupation that nursing assistants take great pride in.

Nursing assistants employed in nursing care facilities in particular are often the principal caregivers, having far more contact with residents than other members of the staff. Because some residents may stay in a nursing care facility for months or even years, assistants develop ongoing relationships with them and interact with them and their families in a positive, caring way.

Nursing assistants held approximately 1.4 million jobs in 2002. Around two in five nursing aides worked in nursing care facilities, and about one-fourth worked in hospitals. Most full-time nursing assistants work about forty hours a week, but because patients need care twenty-four hours a day, some work evenings, nights, weekends, and holidays. Many work part-time. Working as a nursing assistant is an excellent means of entry into the world of work. The flexibility of night and weekend hours also provides high school and college students a chance to work during the school year.

Persons wanting to work as nursing assistants should be tactful, patient, understanding, emotionally stable, and dependable and should have a desire to help people. They also should be able to work as part of a team, have good communication skills, and be willing to perform repetitive, routine tasks.

Assistants must be in good health because of the constant contact they have with people whose immune systems are compromised. A physical examination, including state-regulated tests such as those for tuberculosis, is usually required for employment and is often provided by the employer. Nursing assistants spend many hours standing and walking, and they often face heavy workloads. Because they may have to move patients in and out of bed or help patients stand or walk, nursing assistants must guard against back injury. They also face hazards from minor infections and major diseases, such as hepatitis, but can avoid infections by following proper procedures.

What Nursing Assistants Do

Nursing assistants, also known as nursing aides, geriatric assistants, unlicensed assistive personnel, or hospital attendants, perform routine tasks under the supervision of nursing and medical staff. They answer patients' call lights, deliver messages, serve meals, make beds, and help patients eat, dress, and bathe. Assistants observe patients' physical, mental, and emotional conditions and report any change to the nursing or medical staff. In addition, nursing assistants do the following:

- Provide skin care to patients
- Take vital signs such as temperature, pulse rate, respiration rate, and blood pressure
- Help patients get in and out of bed and walk
- Escort patients to operating and examining rooms

- Empty bedpans and change soiled linen
- Keep patients' rooms neat, set up equipment, store and move supplies
- Assist with some procedures

Training and Education

In many cases, neither a high school diploma nor previous work experience is necessary for a job as a nursing assistant. A few employers, however, and hospitals in particular, require some training or experience. Nursing care facilities often hire inexperienced workers who must complete a minimum of seventy-five hours of mandatory training and pass a competency evaluation program within four months of their employment.

Nursing assistant training is offered in high schools, vocational-technical centers, some nursing care facilities, and some community colleges. Courses cover body mechanics, nutrition, anatomy and physiology, infection control, communication skills, and residents' rights. Personal care skills, such as how to help patients bathe, eat, and groom, also are taught.

Some employers other than nursing care facilities provide classroom instruction for newly hired assistants, while others rely exclusively on informal on-the-job instruction from a licensed nurse or an experienced nursing assistant. Such training may last several days to a few months. From time to time, assistants also may attend lectures, workshops, and in-service training.

Opportunities for advancement within this field are limited. To enter other health occupations, assistants generally need additional formal training. Some employers and unions provide opportunities by simplifying the educational paths to advancement. Gaining experience as an assistant is one way that individuals decide whether to pursue a career in the health care field.

Licensing and Certification

Assistants who complete educational programs are certified and placed on the state registry of nursing assistants.

Earnings

Median hourly earnings of nursing assistants were $9.59 in 2002. The middle 50 percent earned between $8.06 and $11.39 an hour. The lowest 10 percent earned less than $6.98, and the highest 10 percent earned more than $13.54 an hour. Median hourly earnings in the industries employing the largest numbers of nursing assistants in 2002 were as follows:

Employment services	$11.38
Local government	$10.33
General medical and surgical hospitals	$10.09
Nursing care facilities	$9.27
Community care facilities for the elderly	$8.98

Nursing assistants in hospitals generally receive at least one week's paid vacation after one year of service. Paid holidays and sick leave, hospital and medical benefits, extra pay for late-shift work, and pension plans also are available to many hospital, and some nursing care facility, employees.

Job Outlook

Numerous job openings for nursing assistants will arise from a combination of fast employment growth and high replacement needs. High replacement needs in this large occupation reflect modest entry requirements, low pay, high physical and emotional demands, and lack of opportunities for advancement. For these same reasons, many people are unwilling to perform the kind of work required by the occupation. Therefore, persons who are interested in, and suited for, this work should have excellent job opportunities.

According to the Bureau of Labor Statistics, overall employment of nursing assistants is projected to grow faster than the average for all occupations through the year 2012. This is in response to an increasing emphasis on rehabilitation and the long-term care needs of an increasing elderly population. Financial pressures on hospitals to discharge patients as soon as possible should produce more admissions to nursing care facilities. Modern medical technology also will increase the employment of nursing assistants, because, as the technology saves and extends more lives, it increases the need for long-term care provided by assistants.

Home Health Assistant

The duties of home health assistants are similar to those of nursing assistants—they are, in fact, a category of nursing assistant—but they work in patients' homes or residential care facilities. Because they work in people's homes, these workers must be honest and discreet.

Most home health assistants work with elderly or disabled persons who need more extensive care than family or friends can provide. Some help discharged hospital patients who have relatively short-term needs. Home health assistants may go to the same patient's home for months or even years, so they may develop strong relationships with their patients. However, most home health assistants work with a number of different patients, each job lasting a few hours, days, or weeks, and they often visit multiple patients on the same day.

Home health assistants generally work alone, with periodic visits by their supervisor. They receive detailed instructions explaining when to visit patients and what services to perform. They are individually responsible for getting to patients' homes, and they may spend a good portion of the working day traveling from one patient to another. Because mechanical lifting devices available in institutional settings are seldom available in patients' homes, home health assistants are particularly susceptible to injuries resulting from overexertion when they assist patients, so they must be extremely careful when lifting and moving patients not to injure themselves.

In home health agencies, a registered nurse, physical therapist, or social worker assigns specific duties and supervises home health assistants, who keep records of the services they perform and record patients' conditions and progress. They report changes in patients' conditions to the supervisor or case manager.

According to the Bureau of Labor Statistics, home health assistants held roughly 580,000 jobs in 2002. Most home health assistants (about one-third) were employed by home health care services.

What Home Health Assistants Do

Under the direction of nursing or medical staff, home health assistants provide health-related services, such as administering oral medications. Like nursing assistants, home health assistants may check patients' pulse rates, temperatures, and respiration rates; help with simple prescribed exercises; keep patients' rooms neat; and help patients move from bed, bathe, dress, and groom. Occasionally, they change nonsterile dressings, give massages and alcohol rubs, or assist with braces and artificial limbs. Experienced home health assistants also may assist with medical equipment such as ventilators, which help patients breathe.

Training and Education

The federal government has guidelines for home health assistants whose employers receive reimbursement from Medicare. Federal law requires home health assistants to pass a competency test covering twelve areas: communication skills; documentation of patient status and care provided; reading and recording of vital signs; basic infection control procedures; basic body functions; maintenance of a healthy environment; emergency procedures; physical, emotional, and developmental characteristics of patients; personal hygiene and grooming; safe transfer techniques; normal range of motion and positioning; and basic nutrition.

A home health assistant may receive training before taking the competency test. Federal law suggests at least seventy-five hours of classroom and practical training, supervised by a registered nurse. Training and testing programs may be offered by the employing agency but must meet the standards of the Center for Medicare and Medicaid Services. Training programs vary with state regulations.

Licensing and Certification

The National Association for Home Care and Hospice offers national certification for home health assistants. The certification is a voluntary demonstration that the individual has met industry standards.

Earnings

Median hourly earnings of home health assistants were $8.70 in 2002. The middle 50 percent earned between $7.54 and $10.37 an hour. The lowest 10 percent earned less than $6.56, and the highest 10 percent earned more than $12.34 an hour. Median hourly earnings in the industries employing the largest numbers of home health assistants in 2002 were as follows:

Employment services	$9.21
Residential mental retardation, mental health, and substance abuse facilities	$8.91
Home health care services	$8.46
Community care facilities for the elderly	$8.36
Individual and family services	$8.20

Home health assistants receive slight pay increases with experience and added responsibility. Usually, they are paid only for the time worked in the home; normally, they are not paid for travel time between jobs. Most employers hire only on-call hourly workers and provide no benefits.

Job Outlook

Employment of home health assistants is expected to grow the fastest of all forms of nursing assistants, as a result of both growing demand for home health care services from an aging population and efforts to contain health care costs by moving patients out of hospitals and nursing care facilities as quickly as possible. Consumer preference for care in the home and improvements in medical technologies for in-home treatment also will contribute to faster-than-average employment growth for home health assistants.

8

PARAPROFESSIONALS IN DENTISTRY

DENTISTS DIAGNOSE, PREVENT, and treat problems involving the teeth or mouth tissue. They remove decay, fill cavities, examine x-rays, place protective plastic sealants on children's teeth, straighten teeth, and repair fractured teeth. They also perform corrective surgery on gums and supporting bones to treat gum diseases. Dentists extract teeth and make models and measurements for dentures to replace missing teeth. They provide instruction on diet, brushing, flossing, the use of fluorides, and other aspects of dental care. They also administer anesthetics and write prescriptions for antibiotics and other medications. Dentists use a variety of equipment, including x-ray machines, drills, and instruments such as mouth mirrors, probes, forceps, brushes, and scalpels.

Most dentists are general practitioners, handling a variety of dental needs, yet some practice in any of nine specialty areas. Orthodontists, the largest group of specialists, straighten teeth by applying pressure to the teeth with braces or retainers. The next largest group, oral and maxillofacial surgeons, operates on the mouth and jaws. The remainder may specialize as pediatric dentists (focusing on dentistry for children); periodontists (treating gums and bone supporting the teeth); prosthodontists (replacing missing teeth with permanent fixtures, such as crowns and bridges, or removable fixtures, such as dentures); endodontists (performing root canal therapy); public-health dentists (promoting good dental health and preventing dental diseases within the community); oral pathologists (studying oral diseases); or oral and maxillofacial radiologists (diagnosing diseases in the head and neck through the use of imaging technologies).

A dentist's office is almost invariably a busy place, and the chances are that in any dentist's office, you will find between two to five people employed. All dentists typically employ and supervise one or more dental hygienists, dental assistants, dental laboratory technicians, and receptionists. These workers may wear similar jackets and may look alike, but their duties vary considerably as will be seen in this chapter, which focuses on three different dental paraprofessionals—the dental assistant, the dental hygienist, and the dental laboratory technician.

Dental Assistant

Like their equivalents in medicine (medical assistants), dental assistants might be described as the dentist's first assistant. They are an indispensable aspect of any modern dental practice. Duties of dental assistants encompass both working with patients and administrative and clerical functions. Their work area is usually near the dental chair so that they can arrange instruments, materials, and medication and hand them to the dentist when needed. Dental

assistants must wear gloves, masks, eyewear, and protective cloth-
ing to protect themselves and their patients from infectious diseases.
Following safety procedures also minimizes the risks associated with
the use of x-ray machines, another aspect of the dental assistant's
job.

According to the Bureau of Labor Statistics, dental assistants
held about 266,000 jobs in 2002. Almost all jobs for dental assistants were in offices of dentists. A small number of jobs were in
offices of physicians, educational services, and hospitals. About a
third of dental assistants worked part-time, sometimes in more than
one dental office. About half of dental assistants have a thirty-five-
to forty-hour workweek, which may include work on Saturdays or
evenings, since many dentist offices stay open to accommodate
both adults who work nine-to-five jobs and kids who are in school
during the week.

What Dental Assistants Do

Dental assistants perform a variety of patient care, office, and laboratory duties. They work chair-side, as dentists examine and treat
patients. They make patients as comfortable as possible in the dental chair, prepare them for treatment, and obtain their dental
records. Assistants hand instruments and materials to dentists and
keep patients' mouths dry and clear by using suction or other
devices. Although the specific duties performed by the dental assistant vary with the dental practice and the laws of the state in which
the practice is located, generally the patient care tasks that a dental
assistant handles include the following:

- Taking and developing dental radiographs (x-rays)
- Obtaining the patient's medical history and taking blood
  pressure and pulse

- Developing infection control procedures and preparing and sterilizing instruments and equipment
- Providing patients with instructions following surgery or other dental treatments, such as the placement of a restoration (or filling)
- Preparing materials for impressions of patients' teeth for study casts (or models of teeth)
- Removing sutures
- Removing the excess cement used in the filling process
- Applying topical anesthetics to gums or cavity-preventive agents to teeth
- Placing rubber dams on the teeth to isolate them for individual treatment

In addition to all of these duties involving patients, a dental assistant may also handle a variety of administrative duties in the office such as:

- Performing office management tasks involving the use of a computer
- Contacting patients and suppliers, scheduling appointments, answering the telephone, handling the patient billing, and ordering supplies
- Assisting in all dental specialties, including orthodontics (straightening teeth with braces and corrective devices), pediatric dentistry (for children), periodontics (pertaining to tissue and structure surrounding the teeth), and oral surgery (the extraction of teeth)

Finally, those with laboratory duties make casts of the teeth and mouth from impressions, clean and polish removable appliances, and make temporary crowns.

Training and Education

For years dental assistants, like medical assistants, were trained on the job. But because of the increasing complexities of the job and ever-increasing need to focus on professional duties, dental assistants are now almost always graduates of accredited programs and can take examinations for certification, as do medical assistants. Today, dental-assisting programs are offered by community and junior colleges, trade schools, technical institutes, and the armed forces.

Nearly all of the 259 dental assisting programs accredited by the American Dental Association's (ADA) Commission on Dental Accreditation take nine to eleven months of full-time study to complete and result in a certificate or diploma. A few schools offer accelerated courses, training via distance education (online or through satellite or outlying sites of various schools), and other programs for part-time working students or stay-at-home mothers and fathers. A few two-year programs are offered in community colleges that award an associate degree. A number of private vocational schools offer four- to six-month courses in dental assisting, but the Commission on Dental Accreditation does not accredit these programs, which means that employers may be less likely to hire this candidate over one who attended an accredited program. (To locate an accredited program, search the ADA's website at ada.org.)

All programs require at least a high school diploma or its equivalent, and a few require computer-related or science prerequisite courses to be admitted. Useful high school courses include mathematics, chemistry, biology, and computer or office skills. In addition, a personal interview and a physical and dental examination may be required.

The curriculum includes both classroom and lab work and preclinical instruction in dental assisting skills. Students may find work in dental schools, clinics, and, in some cases, dental offices, as part of the training. A typical curriculum in a dental assistant program would include: biological sciences, including human biology, microbiology, and nutrition; dental sciences, including dental materials, oral anatomy, physiology, and oral pathology and therapeutics; dental assisting, including principles of chair-side assisting and practice management; and general studies, such as communications and psychology.

Without further education, advancement opportunities are limited in this field. Some dental assistants become office managers, dental-assisting instructors, or dental product sales representatives. Others go back to school to become dental hygienists. For many, this entry-level occupation provides basic training and experience and serves as a stepping-stone to more highly skilled and better paying jobs.

Licensing and Certification

With two years of on-the-job experience and completion of a dental assisting program, you are eligible to take the examinations given by the Dental Assisting National Board (DANB) that can result in certification. Several certificates awarded include: certified dental assistant, certified oral and maxillofacial surgery assistant, certified dental practice management assistant, and certified orthodontic assistant. Certificates are renewable annually by completing a continuing education requirement.

As an alternative to DANB certification, the American Medical Technologists (AMT) also offers certification for dental assistants. Those dental assistants certified by the AMT are designated Registered Dental Assistant, RDA (AMT). In addition, the AMT also offers the Dental Assisting Radiological Certificate for those who have proven their competency in the radiological area of dental assisting, which allows them to work with x-rays. The completion of the Radiation Health and Safety examination offered by the DANB meets standards in more than thirty states, although some states require the completion of a state-approved course in radiology as well.

Certification is not always required to find a job, but it does show that you have achieved a certain level of competence in dental assisting and can considerably improve your chances of finding initial employment. It also can help you find a job if you should move from one section of the country to another.

Some states require that you pass a certification exam for that state before you can perform specific tasks as a dental assistant. As dental assistants assume greater patient care responsibility, more and more states will require certification.

Earnings

Earnings for dental assistants vary from employer to employer, but educational background, on-the-job experience, and the specific duties for which a dental assistant is responsible will influence salary expectations. Geographic location, too, is another factor that can affect earnings.

In general, dental assistant pay is equal to that of other health care personnel with similar training and experience, such as medical assistants and physical therapy assistants. According to the Bureau of Labor Statistics, median hourly earnings of dental assistants were $13.10 in 2002. The middle 50 percent earned between $10.35 and $16.20 an hour. The lowest 10 percent earned less than $8.45, and the highest 10 percent earned more than $19.41 an hour.

In addition, many dental assistants receive benefit packages including health and disability insurance, reimbursement of fees for joining professional organizations, allowances for uniforms, paid vacations, and last but not least, dental coverage!

Job Outlook

According to the Bureau of Labor Statistics, employment is expected to grow much faster than the average for all occupations through the year 2012. In fact, the job of dental assistant is expected to be one of the fastest-growing occupations through the year 2012. So, to put it simply, the future for dental assistants looks very promising for several reasons: First, more and more workers are covered by dental insurance plans and can therefore afford dental services. Second, the public is increasingly aware of the importance of dental care. Finally, younger dentists just opening their practices as well as older dentists who are increasingly aware of the importance of competent dental assistants are spurring the demand for more dental assistants.

Your best bet for obtaining employment is in a private dental office, but jobs also can be found in hospital dental services, government services (civilian or military), dental assisting educational programs, public health dentistry, dental school clinics, and insurance companies as processors of dental claims.

Dental Hygienist

Both dental assistants and dental hygienists support the dentist in providing dental care to patients, but the duties performed by the dental hygienist are generally more complex and require more training than those handled by the dental assistant. In a manner of speaking, the dental hygienist is one step up the career ladder from the dental assistant. There may be some overlap in what both the dental hygienist and the dental assistant do, but the overall work of the hygienist carries greater responsibilities and, in turn, commands greater monetary compensation. Perhaps the primary difference between the work of a dental hygienist and that of a dental assistant is that the tasks of the former are more directed to patient care and oral hygiene and less to administrative tasks.

According to the Bureau of Labor Statistics, dental hygienists held about 148,000 jobs in 2002. Because multiple jobholding is common in this field, the number of jobs exceeds the number of hygienists. More than half of all dental hygienists worked part-time—fewer than thirty-five hours a week. Almost all of these jobs were in offices of dentists; only a very small number worked for employment services or in offices of physicians. However, of those not working in dentists' offices, dental hygienists worked as educators, researchers, administrators, managers, preventive program developers, consumer advocates, sales and marketing managers, editors, and consultants. Clinical dental hygienists may work in a variety of health care settings such as private dental offices, schools, public health clinics, hospitals, managed care organizations, correctional institutions, or nursing homes.

What Dental Hygienists Do

The main part of a dental hygienist's job is to teach patients how to practice good oral hygiene and provide other preventive dental care. Hygienists examine patients' teeth and gums and record the presence of diseases or abnormalities. In some states, hygienists administer anesthetics; place and carve filling materials, temporary fillings, and periodontal dressings; remove sutures; and smooth and polish metal restorations. Although hygienists may not diagnose diseases, they can prepare clinical and laboratory diagnostic tests for the dentist to interpret. Hygienists sometimes work chair-side with the dentist during treatment.

Dental hygienists help patients develop and maintain good oral health by explaining the relationship between diet and oral health or informing patients how to select toothbrushes and show them how to brush and floss their teeth. Dental hygienists use hand and rotary instruments and ultrasonic equipment to clean and polish teeth, syringes with needles to administer local anesthetics, and models of teeth to explain oral hygiene. The duties of a dental hygienist cover a wide range of services, including:

- Patient screening services such as assessing oral health conditions, review of health history, oral cancer screening, head and neck inspection, dental charting, and taking blood pressure and pulse
- Taking and developing dental x-rays
- Removing calculus and plaque (hard and soft deposits) from all teeth surfaces
- Applying preventive materials to guard against plaque (sealants and fluorides)
- Teaching patients appropriate oral hygiene strategies to maintain oral health (including toothbrushing, flossing, and nutritional counseling)
- Making impressions of patients' teeth for study casts (models of teeth used by dentists to evaluate patient treatment needs)
- Performing documentation and office management activities

Although these are the primary duties of dental hygienists, there are many others, depending on the dental practice and the state.

Flexible scheduling is a distinctive, and to some, very attractive feature of this job. Full-time, part-time, evening, and weekend schedules are widely available. Dentists frequently hire hygienists to work only two or three days a week, so hygienists may hold jobs in more than one dental office. This is especially attractive for those who are raising families or pursuing additional education.

Dental hygienists work in clean, well-lighted offices. Important health safeguards include strict adherence to proper radiological procedures, and the use of appropriate protective devices when administering anesthetic gas. Dental hygienists also wear safety glasses, surgical masks, and gloves to protect themselves and patients from infectious diseases.

Training and Education

Dental hygienists have never been trained on the job. Even in Alabama, where there is a preceptorship program (where the hygienist is trained by a supervising worker), students receive some formal classroom education. In 2002, the Commission on Dental Accreditation accredited about 265 programs in dental hygiene. (To locate an accredited program, search the ADA's website at ada.org.)

There are three kinds of educational programs for dental hygienists: most schools offer an associate (two-year) degree, a few offer a bachelor's degree, and six universities offer a master's degree. The associate degree or certificate of dental hygiene, involving two years of study, is the minimum educational requirement for employment in a private dental practice. A bachelor's and sometimes master's degree are required for positions involving research, teaching, or working with patients in public or school programs.

Most dental hygiene programs require at least one year of college study before entering the program, but some require two years of college. Each school will have specific admissions requirements that should be researched in advance. Admission to most dental hygiene programs is competitive, and to be accepted, a high school diploma and a solid background in math and science is a must.

The dental hygiene curriculum is based on a variety of courses involving classroom instruction as well as laboratory work and exposure to patients. Courses offered usually include anatomy, physiology, chemistry, microbiology, pharmacology, nutrition, histology (the study of tissue structure), periodontology (the study of gum diseases), pathology, dental radiology, and dental materials.

The clinical aspect of the program—in which you work with patients—includes supervised practical dental hygiene experiences plus such courses as chair-side dental assisting, dental health education, community health, and so forth. In addition, liberal arts courses in English, psychology, sociology, and speech are helpful.

Licensing and Certification

Unlike dental assistants, dental hygienists must be licensed by the state in which they practice. To qualify for licensure, a candidate must graduate from an accredited dental hygiene school and pass both a written and clinical examination. The American Dental Association Joint Commission on National Dental Examinations administers the written examination, which is accepted by all states and the District of Columbia. State or regional testing agencies administer the clinical examination. In addition, most states require an examination on the legal aspects of dental hygiene practice. Alabama allows candidates to take its examinations if they have been trained through a state-regulated on-the-job program in a dentist's office.

Earnings

According to the Bureau of Labor Statistics, median hourly earnings of dental hygienists were $26.59 in 2002. The middle 50 percent earned between $21.96 and $32.48 an hour. The lowest 10 percent earned less than $17.34, and the highest 10 percent earned more than $39.24 an hour. Earnings vary, of course, depending on the employer, geographical location, level of education, and experience. Those working in private dental offices may be paid on an hourly, daily, salary, or commission basis or a combination of salary and commission.

Benefits vary a lot depending upon location and whether the work is full- or part-time. Dental hygienists working for public health agencies, school systems, or the federal government usually enjoy substantial benefits.

Job Outlook

According to the Bureau of Labor Statistics, employment of dental hygienists is expected to grow much faster than the average for all occupations through 2012 in response to increasing demand for dental care and the greater utilization of hygienists to perform services previously performed by dentists. This will be one of the fastest-growing occupations through the year 2012.

Population growth and greater retention of natural teeth will stimulate demand for dental hygienists. Older dentists, who have been less likely to employ dental hygienists, are leaving the occupation and will be replaced by recent graduates, who are more likely to employ one or even two hygienists. In addition, as dentists' workloads increase, they are expected to hire more hygienists to perform preventive dental care, such as cleaning, so that they may devote their own time to more profitable procedures.

Dental Laboratory Technician

The dental laboratory technician, also known as a dental technician, is somewhat of an artist, requiring an artist's creativity and touch as he or she constructs a variety of dental appliances to the dentist's specifications or prescription. It is work that is highly precise and complex, involving several stages of effort. In addition, the dental technician must possess skills in the use of small hand instruments and in accuracy, artistic ability, and attention to minute detail. The work is extremely delicate and time-consuming.

While most dental laboratory technicians work in dental laboratories, some work right in the dentist's office, where they are readily accessible. They usually have their own workbenches, which can be equipped with Bunsen burners, grinding and polishing equipment, and hand instruments, such as wax spatulas and wax carvers. Some technicians have computer-aided milling equipment to assist them with creating artificial teeth.

Dental laboratory technicians held about 47,000 jobs in 2002. Around seven out of ten jobs were in medical equipment and supply manufacturing laboratories, which usually are small, privately owned businesses with fewer than five employees. However, some laboratories are large; a few employ more than fifty technicians. As mentioned, some dental laboratory technicians work in offices of dentists, while others work for hospitals providing dental services, including U.S. Department of Veterans Affairs hospitals. Some technicians work in dental laboratories in their homes, in addition to their regular jobs. Salaried technicians usually work forty hours a week, but self-employed technicians frequently work longer hours.

What Dental Technicians Do

Dental laboratory technicians fill prescriptions from dentists for crowns, bridges, dentures, and other dental prosthetics. First, dentists send a specification of the item to be manufactured, along with an impression (mold) of the patient's mouth or teeth. Then, dental laboratory technicians create a model of the patient's mouth by pouring plaster into the impression and allowing it to set. Next, they place the model on an apparatus that mimics the bite and movement of the patient's jaw. The model serves as the basis of the prosthetic device. Technicians examine the model, noting the size and shape of the adjacent teeth, as well as gaps within the gum line. Based upon these observations and the dentist's specifications, dental technicians build and shape a wax tooth or teeth model, using small hand instruments called wax spatulas and wax carvers. They use this wax model to cast the metal framework for the prosthetic device.

After the wax tooth has been formed, dental technicians pour the cast and form the metal and, using small handheld tools, prepare the surface to allow the metal and porcelain to bond. They then apply porcelain in layers, to arrive at the precise shape and color of a tooth. Technicians place the tooth in a porcelain furnace to bake the porcelain onto the metal framework, and then adjust the shape and color, with subsequent grinding and addition of porcelain to achieve a sealed finish. The final product is a nearly exact replica of the lost tooth or teeth.

In some laboratories, technicians perform all stages of the work, whereas in other labs, each technician does only a few. Dental laboratory technicians can specialize in one of five areas: orthodontic appliances, crowns and bridges, complete dentures, partial dentures, or ceramics. Job titles reflect specialization in these areas. For example, technicians who make porcelain and acrylic restorations are called dental ceramists.

Training and Education

Most dental laboratory technicians learn their craft on the job. They begin with simple tasks, such as pouring plaster into an impression, and progress to more complex procedures, such as making porcelain crowns and bridges. Becoming a fully trained technician requires an average of three to four years, depending upon the individual's aptitude and ambition, but it may take a few years more to become an accomplished technician.

Training in dental laboratory technology also is available through community and junior colleges, vocational-technical institutes, and the U.S. armed forces. Formal training programs vary greatly both in length and in the level of skill they impart.

In 2002, twenty-five programs in dental laboratory technology were approved (accredited) by the Commission on Dental Accreditation in conjunction with the American Dental Association. (To locate an accredited program, search the ADA's website at ada.org.) These programs provide classroom instruction in dental materials science, oral anatomy, fabrication procedures, ethics, and related subjects. In addition, each student is given supervised practical experience in a school or an associated dental laboratory. Accredited programs normally take two years to complete and lead to an associate degree. A few programs take about four years to complete and offer a bachelor's degree in dental technology.

Graduates of two-year training programs need additional hands-on experience to become fully qualified. Each dental laboratory owner operates in a different way, and classroom instruction does not necessarily expose students to techniques and procedures favored by individual laboratory owners. Students who have taken enough courses to learn the basics of the craft usually are considered good candidates for training, regardless of whether they have completed a formal program. Many employers will train someone without any classroom experience.

In large dental laboratories, technicians may become supervisors or managers. Experienced technicians may teach or may take jobs with dental suppliers in such areas as product development, marketing, and sales. Still, for most technicians, opening one's own laboratory is the way toward advancement and higher earnings.

High school students interested in becoming dental laboratory technicians should take courses in art, metal and wood shop, drafting, and sciences. Courses in management and business may help those wishing to operate their own laboratories.

Licensing and Certification

Certification, which is optional, is offered by the National Board for Certification in Dental Laboratory Technology in five specialty areas: crown and bridge, ceramics, partial dentures, complete dentures, and orthodontic appliances.

Earnings

What you earn as a dental laboratory technician will depend primarily on your skills and the responsibilities called for in the specific position where you are employed. According to the Bureau of Labor Statistics, median hourly earnings of dental laboratory technicians were $13.70 in 2002. The middle 50 percent earned between $10.51 and $18.40 an hour. The lowest 10 percent earned less than $8.16, and the highest 10 percent earned more than

$23.65 an hour. Median hourly earnings of dental laboratory technicians in 2002 were $13.78 in medical equipment and supplies manufacturing and $12.98 in offices of dentists. Technicians in large laboratories tend to specialize in a few procedures, and, therefore, tend to be paid a lower wage than those employed in small laboratories that perform a variety of tasks. Earnings rise sharply with experience and, in general, dental technicians can expect to earn more if they are self-employed than if they are salaried.

Job Outlook

Job opportunities for dental laboratory technicians should be favorable, despite expected slower-than-average growth in the occupation through the year 2012. Employers have difficulty filling trainee positions, probably because entry-level salaries are relatively low and because the public is not familiar with the occupation.

The overall dental health of the population has improved because of fluoridation of drinking water (which has reduced the incidence of dental cavities) and greater emphasis on preventive dental care since the early 1960s. As a result, full dentures will be less common, as most people will need only a bridge or crown. However, during the last few years, demand has arisen from an aging public that is growing increasingly interested in cosmetic prostheses. For example, many dental laboratories are filling orders for composite fillings that are the same shade of white as natural teeth to replace older, less attractive fillings.

9

PARAPROFESSIONALS IN OPTOMETRY

CHANCES ARE THAT you will find allied health paraprofessionals working in the office of any health and medical professional. The eye care team includes ophthalmologists, nurses, and allied health personnel. Specifically, within allied health, several areas of expertise exist, including optometric assistants and technicians (collectively called paraoptometrics), ophthalmic assistants, ophthalmic technicians/technologists, and orthoptists. This chapter concentrates on the various categories of eye care paraprofessionals, those critical workers who help us see better. Before we begin, we should clarify two very similar and often confused job titles: the ophthalmologist and the optometrist.

This chapter describes various paraprofessionals who work for both the ophthalmologist and the optometrist and, while there are many similarities in their job descriptions, there are also some important differences, which is why it's helpful to understand the distinctions between these two types of "eye doctors." An ophthalmologist is a medical doctor licensed to practice medicine and perform eye surgery. Ophthalmologists examine eyes and prescribe eyeglasses and contact lenses. They treat diseases and injuries of the eyes, and they also perform eye surgery. An optometrist, on the other hand, is not a medical doctor, but has a postbachelor's degree in optometry and is licensed to practice optometry. Optometrists treat patients with vision difficulty, eye disease, and injury. They are educated and licensed to diagnose and treat ocular conditions and are qualified to screen for systemic diseases. Like ophthalmologists, they prescribe eyeglasses, contact lenses, vision therapy, and low-vision aids. They use drugs for diagnosis and treatment of ocular disorders and diseases. They do not perform surgery. In short, the major difference is that the ophthalmologist can perform eye surgery and has a doctorate degree; the optometrist does not.

Optometric Assistant and Technician

More than half the people in the United States wear glasses or contact lenses that correct their vision. To obtain these corrective lenses, they must have an eye or vision examination and a prescription from an optometrist or ophthalmologist. Optometrists conduct the majority of the eye examinations given in the United States, examining patients for poor vision, eye disease, and other ocular disorders. They can also detect early signs of systemic diseases such as diabetes, high blood pressure, and hardening of the arteries. They may refer these patients to internists, neurologists, cardiologists, or family practice physicians. After they test and evaluate a patient's eyes, optometrists may prescribe and supply patients with glasses or contact lenses.

As is true of virtually all other categories of paraprofessionals, optometric assistants and technicians handle the routine tasks presented in an optometrist's office, thus freeing up the optometrist for the more complex aspects of his or her practice. They often work closely with the patients themselves, although usually at the beginning and end of the patient visit. Paraoptometrics work in pleasant, comfortable offices or clinics. There is usually a reception room, an examination room with modern equipment, and a private office. They may work with an optometrist who owns his or her own practice or is in a partnership. Other members of the eye care team may include additional optometric technicians or assistants to help serve patients.

What Optometric Assistants and Technicians Do

Optometric assistants handle mostly administrative tasks, including scheduling appointments, handling bookkeeping, typing and filing, keeping patient records, and maintaining inventories of supplies and materials. In addition, the optometric assistant might help a client choose the most appropriate glasses, adjust them, and answer any questions about the care and maintenance of the new frames. This job tends to be more customer-service oriented, and it requires the ability both to impart information clearly and to interact with a diverse group of people.

Because their training is lengthier and more intensive than that of optometric assistants, optometric technicians are qualified to handle more complex tasks such as conducting simple vision tests, recording eye pressures, taking medical histories, and so on, but this does vary according to the practice.

Other duties typically performed by paraoptometrics include:

- Handling tests of depth perception, color vision, acuity, and visual field
- Performing facial and frame measurements and assisting patients in selecting frames
- Determining the power of old and new lenses
- Ordering lenses prescribed by the optometrist
- Serving as chair-side assistant to record data obtained during the optometrist's examination
- Working with children with visual problems who require visual training
- Providing patients with visual therapy
- Maintaining inventory of materials and cleaning instruments

Training and Education

While most paraoptometrics were at one time trained in the office, as the job has become increasingly complex, few if any optometrists are willing to take the time involved in training paraoptometric personnel. Still, some optometrists do hire personnel who have not graduated from an accredited program so long as they are high school graduates. Increasingly, however, the training function is falling to various community colleges, technical institutes, and colleges of optometry that offer one-year courses to train would-be optometric assistants. Certificates of completion or diplomas are awarded after completion of these programs. There are also two-year programs in community colleges specifically aimed at training the higher-level optometric technicians; these award an associate degree.

As is true of most paraprofessional training programs, courses combine class work with technical studies. They include such courses as physics, biology, algebra, geometry, as well as anatomy and physiology of the eye, vision training exercises to correct eye problems, and contact lens theory and practice. In addition, most programs offer courses in office skills.

To qualify for training as a paraoptometric, you must be a high school graduate or have passed the GED. High school courses that will prove helpful in qualifying for the work are English, math, science, and office skills, especially typing and computers.

Licensing and Certification

Certification is awarded to paraoptometrics through the American Optometric Association's (AOA) Commission on Paraoptometric Certification. This certification is entirely voluntary, but increasingly, optometrists are looking for such certification in hiring and advancing their paraoptometric personnel because it shows that applicants have acquired a higher level of education and skills. The titles and certification levels for paraoptometrics are:

- **Certified Paraoptometric (CPO).** This person has demonstrated an understanding of the concepts used in optometric care. The CPO also has demonstrated competence by a didactic examination and is on-the-job trained. To take the test, applicants must have a minimum of a high school diploma or equivalent as well as a minimum of six months' experience working in the eye care field.
- **Certified Paraoptometric Assistant (CPOA).** This person has demonstrated the ability to apply the concepts used in optometric care. To take the test, applicants must have earned the CPO title and verify at least six months' additional work experience as a CPO, be graduates or students currently enrolled and in good standing in their last semester of study of an optometric assistant program, or have proof of five years or more of on-the-job experience.

• **Certified Paraoptometric Technician (CPOT).** This person has demonstrated the ability to understand, apply, and interrelate the concepts used in optometric care. Similar to the CPOA, to take this test, applicants must earn the CPOA title and have a minimum of six months' additional employment in the field as a CPOA or be a graduate or student currently enrolled and in good standing in the last semester of study of an Accreditation Council on Optometric Education–approved optometric technician program.

Earnings

Your earnings as a paraoptometric will depend upon geographical location, kind of practice, size of practice, and your personal qualifications for either assistant or technician. In general, however, according to the Bureau of Labor Statistics, median annual earnings of optometric technicians were $23,600 in 2002. The middle 50 percent earned between $17,960 and $31,530. Median annual earnings in the industries employing the largest numbers of optometric technicians in 2002 were as follows:

Offices of physicians	$26,250
Health and personal-care stores	$23,860
Offices of other health practitioners	$22,900

Optometric assistants earn slightly less than their more educated counterparts.

Job Outlook

According to the Bureau of Labor Statistics, employment of paraoptometrics is expected to increase about as fast as the average for all occupations through 2012 as demand grows for corrective lenses. The increase in demand is a result of the fact that the number of middle-aged and elderly persons is projected to increase rapidly. Middle age is a time when many individuals use corrective lenses for the first time because of the natural aging of the eye, and elderly persons generally require more vision care than others.

Fashion, too, influences demand. Frames come in a growing variety of styles and colors—encouraging people to buy more than one pair. In addition, demand is expected to grow in response to the availability of new technologies that improve the quality and look of corrective lenses, such as antireflective coatings and bifocal lenses without the line that is visible in old-style bifocals. Improvements in bifocal, extended-wear, and disposable contact lenses also will spur demand.

The need to replace those who leave the occupation will result in additional job openings. Nevertheless, the number of job openings will be limited because the occupation is small. Paraoptometrics are vulnerable to changes in the business cycle, because eyewear purchases often can be deferred for a time, but increasingly the best job opportunities will go to graduates of accredited training programs for both optometric assistants and optometric technicians.

Ophthalmic Assistant, Technician, and Technologist

Like paraoptometrics, ophthalmic assistants, technicians, and technologists are paraprofessionals qualified by their training and experience to perform support services for the medical professional who employs them; in this case, the ophthalmologist. Working under the supervision of the ophthalmologist, they carry out various services involved in the diagnosis and treatment of eye disease.

Although there is some overlapping of duties at the three levels of the paraprofessionals involved—the assistant, technician, and technologist—the duties become increasingly involved and complex as you advance from one level to the next. Clearly, an assistant is the least formally educated worker, and tends to do the more administrative and clerical tasks in an office. A technician receives formal training in an area, in this case in ophthalmology, and is able to perform simple procedures and tests. A technologist has received the most formal training of the three, is able to perform more elaborate tests and diagnostic measures, and may be placed in a supervisory position.

According to a survey conducted in 2000 by the Association of Technical Personnel in Ophthalmology, more than 65 percent of all paraprofessionals in ophthalmology worked in private group practices while more than 13 percent worked in private solo practices. These types of work environments tend to have more routine schedules than hospital settings or multispecialty clinics and the work hours are usually nine to five, although some practices may stay open late a few nights or on Saturdays to accommodate other nine-to-five workers. Ophthalmic technologists working in an ambulatory surgery center usually work mornings and a limited number of days a week.

What Ophthalmic Assistants, Technicians, and Technologists Do

An ophthalmic assistant's job duties, while somewhat restricted, are nevertheless important. The following are a few of the tasks an ophthalmic assistant might perform in a day:

- Measuring visual acuity, with or without eyeglasses
- Obtaining the patient's ophthalmic (eye) history, paying special attention to any eye problems or complaints
- Obtaining other technical measurements, such as sphere, cylinder, and axis of lenses
- Caring for and maintaining eye-care equipment
- Handling minor adjustments and repairs in eyeglasses and ophthalmologic instruments

In addition to the job functions and services listed above, an ophthalmic technician handles more advanced procedures in providing medical care to patients. Some of the duties include the following:

- Measuring for contact lens fittings and instructing patients in the insertion, removal, and care of lenses
- Taking eye smears as specimens for eye culture examinations
- Making comprehensive measurements for ocular mobility
- Handling direct patient care functions including changing of eye dressings, installing eye drops and ointments, administering medications, and instructing patients on home eye care
- Performing advanced maintenance functions of ophthalmic instruments and equipment such as optical alignment and calibration

An ophthalmic technologist is trained to perform additional tasks on an even higher level, requiring greater technical skill. For example, an ophthalmic technologist may carry out certain clinical procedures within specialized areas of ophthalmology, such as assisting in eye surgery or supervising other assistants and technicians. Other jobs might include:

- Testing patients with special instruments such as ultrasound diagnostic equipment to determine extent of eye problems
- Conducting advanced tests for color vision
- Performing ophthalmic clinical photography and fluorescence angiography to get a better picture of the parts of the eye
- Conducting electrophysiological and microbiological procedures for diagnosing disease

Training and Education

Personal skills and interests for excelling in this area include scientific curiosity, sound judgment, a spirit of cooperativeness, maturity, and the quality of accuracy. At least a high school diploma or GED is necessary to qualify for training in this career. Some kind of training is necessary to establish a career in ophthalmic medical assisting. This can be either on-the-job training or a formal training program.

In 2004, there were seventeen programs in ophthalmic medical assisting that were recognized and accredited by the Committee on Accreditation for Ophthalmic Medical Personnel (part of the Joint Commission on Allied Health Personnel in Ophthalmology). Programs last from one to two years and include courses in anatomy and physiology, medical terminology, medical law and ethics, ophthalmic optics, and microbiology. The programs also include clinical training such as visual field testing, contact lenses, ophthalmic surgery, and care and maintenance of ophthalmic equipment. Each program is geared toward one of the three certification levels—ophthalmic assistant, technician, or technologist—so programs vary in intensity and length. (See JCAHPO's website at jcahpo.org/assistan.htm for a complete list of schools.)

In addition to formal programs, the certification described below can be achieved by gaining on-the-job experience working in an ophthalmologist's office and successfully completing an approved home study course. The only home or independent study course recognized and accredited by the Committee on Accreditation for Ophthalmic Medical Personnel as of 2004 is the following:

Ophthalmic Medical Assisting: An Independent Study Course
American Academy of Ophthalmology
Clinical Education Division
Box 7424
San Francisco, CA 94120-7424

Licensing and Certification

The Joint Commission on Allied Health Personnel in Ophthalmology, which is in turn accredited by the National Commission for Certifying Agencies (NCCA), awards credentials to the ophthalmic paraprofessionals at the following three levels:

1. **Certified Ophthalmic Assistant.** This entry-level certification exam tests knowledge of topics such as history taking, basic skills and lensometry (lens fitting), patient services, tonometry (a standard test that determines fluid pressure in the eye), instrument maintenance, and general medical knowledge focusing on the anatomy and physiology of the eye.

2. **Certified Ophthalmic Technician.** This is an intermediate certification that, in addition to the content above, tests for knowledge of clinical optics, basic eye movement, visual fields, contact lenses, ocular pharmacology, and photography.

3. **Certified Ophthalmic Medical Technologist.** This is the advanced certification level that, in addition to topics covered by

the previous two levels of certification, tests for knowledge of topics such as microbiology, color vision, clinical optics, and special instrument and techniques.

Achieving certification as an ophthalmic assistant is required before you can advance to a higher level of certification. Examinations are administered throughout the year at many locations. To maintain certification, you must earn a specific number of JCAHPO-approved continuing education credits, which vary according to the level of certification.

Earnings

What you earn in this field will depend on your level of certification, where you work (in a private office, at a medical school, or in a medical center), the location of the practice, and your own background and experience. According to a survey by the Association of Technical Personnel in Ophthalmology, respondents' answers were nearly split in terms of being paid hourly or on an annual salary. The same survey showed that the average hourly wage range was $16 to $18, the average annual salary range was $50,000 to $54,000, and the full range of salaries went from a low of $20,000 to a high of nearly $70,000. Clearly, the benefits of additional education and training and accumulated on-the-job experience will pay off in this field.

Job Outlook

Employment opportunities are excellent in this field. Ophthalmic medical personnel find jobs in a variety of settings where ophthalmologists practice, including private offices, hospital eye clinics, and university ophthalmology departments. Job satisfaction in this field is favorable and there is not as high a rate of job burnout as with other medical assistants. With the population continuing to age, the need for eye care is expected to increase and the demand for well-trained ophthalmic medical personnel will continue to expand.

Orthoptist

Occupying a very special niche in the entire array of eye care paraprofessionals is the orthoptist. The focus of this career is the evaluation and treatment of disorders of vision, eye movement, and eye alignment of children and adults. The primary concern of the orthoptist would be treating and diagnosing eye conditions affecting eye mobility and binocular vision (using both eyes at the same time to see). Working under the supervision of the ophthalmologist, the orthoptist primarily works with children suffering from strabismus, otherwise known as crossed eyes. Other eye conditions treated by the orthoptist include amblyopia (lazy eye), which is most commonly seen in children but affects adults as well, and nystagmus, a condition in which the eye appears to be vibrating, a condition that can be normal in adolescents but is abnormal in adults.

There are only an estimated three hundred people working in the United States in this specialized field, which has been in existence for nearly fifty years. Orthoptics is a field with opportunities in a variety of clinical settings, including private ophthalmology practices, hospitals, and medical universities. Orthoptists can work directly in patient care or they can work in the fields of academics and clinical research. As a consultant, an orthoptist may travel to several offices or clinics to see patients or participate as a professional advisor to community agencies concerned with vision. In addition, orthoptists may serve as directors or advisors of state and local vision screening programs.

What Orthoptists Do

Orthoptists help persons with correctable problems with focusing to develop and use binocular vision (focusing of both eyes). After performing various testing procedures, the orthoptist formulates a diagnosis and nonsurgical treatment plan for the patient. This information is then entered into the patient's medical record. The orthoptist is the liaison between the ophthalmologist and the patient and as such assists in the explanation and carrying out of a patient's individual treatment plan, including education regarding any surgery the ophthalmologist may have to perform. In addition, orthoptists do the following:

- Measure a patient's visual acuity, focusing ability, and motor movement of eyes
- Help a patient move, focus, and coordinate both eyes to aid in visual development
- Develop a patient's visual skills, ability to discriminate between objects, and depth perception, using glasses and prisms
- Instruct adult patients or parents of young patients how to use corrective methods at home

Training and Education

A bachelor's degree is required to enter an orthoptic training program. It is helpful, but not necessary, to have a basic science or health care background. Training involves attending one of fifteen two-year programs accredited by the American Orthoptic Council (AOC). Some students, who already have JCAHPO certification as an ophthalmic technician or technologist, may be able to receive advanced standing status and study for one year instead of two. Curriculums combine classroom lectures with the study of journal publications and usually cover anatomy, neuroanatomy, physiology, pharmacology, ophthalmic optics, and diagnostic testing and measurement. Check out the American Association of Certified Orthoptists and the American Orthoptic Council's jointly operated website at orthoptics.org for a complete list of accredited schools.

High school and college courses to take in preparation for entrance into an orthoptics program include biology, anatomy, optics, and child development.

Licensing and Certification

Upon completion of the program, students must pass a written and oral or practical examination given by the AOC. Written exams are given once a year, in June. Oral exams are conducted every fall and involve examining a patient and answering questions covering the entire field of study. Certification is awarded upon passing this exam. Recertification requires proof of continuing education on an annual basis.

Earnings

As is true of all paramedical careers, your earnings will depend upon where you work—in a private office, public clinic, or a military facility; the section of the country in which you work; and your background and experience.

In recent years, starting salaries for orthoptists have ranged from $19,000 to $23,000 a year, but with experience and proven ability, you can earn well in excess of $50,000 a year.

Job Outlook

This is a field in which the demand for qualified personnel is far outstripping the availability of trained workers. With the aging of the population, which will be reflected in increased demand for optical services, the demand for skilled orthoptists should grow even sharper.

10

Paraprofessionals in Physical and Occupational Therapy

Physical and occupational therapy are very much "hands-on" in nature. Those paraprofessionals who choose to pursue a career in one of these areas will be able to make a positive and constructive impact on the patients they work with.

Physical Therapist Assistant

As is true of just about all medical and health care professionals, physical therapists are busy people. To enable them to use their time most effectively and to tend to the needs of ever-increasing numbers of patients, they rely on the paraprofessional—in this case, the physical therapist assistant. Physical therapist assistants perform components of physical therapy procedures and related tasks selected by a supervising physical therapist. These workers assist physical therapists in providing services that help improve mobility, relieve pain, and prevent or limit permanent physical disabilities of patients suffering from injuries or disease. Patients include accident victims and individuals with disabling conditions such as low-back pain, arthritis, heart disease, fractures, head injuries, and cerebral palsy.

Don't confuse the physical therapist assistant with the physical therapist aide. Assistants are for the most part trained in various accredited educational programs, while aides are trained on the job and work under a physical therapist or a physical therapist assistant. Physical therapist aides are responsible for keeping the treatment area clean and organized and for preparing for each patient's therapy. When patients need assistance moving to or from a treatment area, aides push them in a wheelchair or provide them with a shoulder to lean on. Because they are not licensed, aides do not perform the clinical tasks of a physical therapist assistant.

Physical therapist assistants held about 50,000 jobs in 2002, working alongside physical therapists in a variety of settings. Almost three-fourths of all jobs were in hospitals or in offices of other health practitioners (which includes offices of physical therapists). Others worked primarily in nursing care facilities, offices of physicians, home health care services, and outpatient care centers. The hours and days that physical therapist assistants work vary with the facility and with whether they are full- or part-time employees. Many outpatient physical therapy offices and clinics have evening and weekend hours, to help coincide with patients' personal schedules.

Physical therapist assistants need a moderate degree of strength because of the physical exertion required in assisting patients with their treatment. In some cases, assistants need to lift and move patients. Constant kneeling, stooping, and standing for long periods also are part of the job.

What Physical Therapist Assistants Do

The nature and extent of the duties of physical therapist assistants are determined by the institution where they work and the supervising physical therapist. Generally, the physical therapist is concerned with the diagnosis and evaluation of the patient to be treated, as well as the development of the treatment plan. Such treatment plans often include giving tests to determine loss of muscle strength, motor development, functional ability, capacity for respiration, and circulation efficiency.

Physical therapist assistants perform a variety of tasks, including implementing the tests and treatments outlined by the physical therapist. Physical therapist assistants record the patient's responses to treatment and report the outcome of each treatment to the physical therapist. Components of treatment procedures performed by these workers, under the direction and supervision of physical therapists, include the following:

- Rendering exercises, massages, electrical stimulation, paraffin baths, hot/cold packs, traction, and ultrasound to help patients regain the use of their limbs
- Assisting in carrying out and evaluating tests and more complex treatment procedures
- Observing and reporting patients' progress
- Administering traction to relieve neck and back pain
- Using intermittent and stationary traction equipment
- Fitting patients for adjustments and training them in the use of orthopedic and supportive devices such as canes, crutches, walkers, and wheelchairs
- Orienting new physical therapist assistants to the job

- Exchanging information with the physical therapy staff on patient treatment plans, progress, and problems
- Handling such clerical duties as taking inventory, ordering supplies, answering the phone, and taking messages
- Evaluating patients' range of motion, length and girth of limbs, and vital signs to measure the effectiveness of various treatments or to assist the physical therapist in patient evaluation

Training and Education

According to the American Physical Therapy Association (APTA), as of 2003 there were 245 accredited physical therapist assistant programs in the United States. (See the APTA's website for a complete list of schools at apta.org/education/pta_programs.) These programs, which ordinarily run for two years, are offered in community and junior colleges, as well as in four-year colleges and universities and at medical centers. The programs are divided between a year of academic study and working with patients during the second year. Academic courses include algebra, geometry, physiology, biology, chemistry, and psychology. Before beginning clinical work, many schools require that students complete a semester of anatomy and physiology and are certified in CPR and first aid. Admission to physical therapist assistant training programs is very competitive, so there may be a long waiting list to get in. It is therefore desirable to contact schools well in advance for information regarding admission requirements, costs, and any financial assistance available.

In high school, taking courses in health, biology, mathematics, psychology, physical education, and computer science will help prepare for college courses leading to a degree.

Licensing and Certification

Licensure or registration is currently required in forty-one states. To qualify for licensure, applicants must be a graduate of an accredited program and pass a written examination given by the state; in some cases, applicants must have logged a minimum number of clinical hours. But certification requirements do vary from state to state, so it is best to contact the state licensing board for its specific requirements. Requirements for renewal of certification also varies by state; most high school and college career counseling offices and resource centers or the state licensure board can provide more information on this.

Earnings

Median annual earnings of physical therapist assistants were $36,080 in 2002. The middle 50 percent earned between $30,260 and $42,780. The lowest 10 percent earned less than $23,530, and the highest 10 percent earned more than $48,910. Median annual earnings of physical therapist assistants in 2002 were $35,870 in general medical and surgical hospitals and $35,750 in offices of other health practitioners. Salaries vary according to geographical location, work settings, and, of course, background and experience.

Job Outlook

According to the Bureau of Labor Statistics, employment of physical therapist assistants is expected to grow much faster than the average through the year 2012. The impact of proposed federal legislation imposing limits on reimbursement for therapy services may adversely affect the short-term job outlook for physical therapist assistants. However, over the long run, demand for physical therapist assistants will continue to rise, in accordance with growth in the number of individuals with disabilities or limited function. Elderly persons are especially vulnerable to chronic and debilitating conditions requiring treatment by physical therapists and their assistants. Also a factor in the need for treatment and therapy is the aging of the baby boomers; as they approach the age of higher incidence of heart attacks and strokes, there will be an increased need for cardiac and physical treatment. The increased participation of the population in sports and physical fitness activities will further accelerate the demand for physical therapist assistants to treat and help prevent knee, leg, shoulder, back, and other injuries involving the musculoskeletal system. In addition, physical therapists are expected to increasingly utilize assistants to reduce the cost of physical therapy services. Once a patient is evaluated and a treatment plan is designed by the physical therapist, the physical therapist assistant can provide many aspects of treatment, as prescribed by the therapist.

Occupational Therapy Assistant

Occupational therapists have nothing to do with helping a patient find employment; they focus on assisting patients to function to the best of their ability in the tasks of everyday living. The goal of occupational therapy is to help patients learn the functions that allow them to live as independent human beings: learning, for example, how to dress and cook, how to pick up objects, how to button coats and clothes, or how to tie a tie, often while at the same time striving to overcome any temporary bilateral paralysis.

Occupational therapist assistants work under the direction of occupational therapists to provide rehabilitative services to persons with mental, physical, emotional, or developmental impairments. The ultimate goal is to improve a client's quality of life. For example, occupational therapist assistants help injured workers reenter the labor force by teaching them how to compensate for lost motor skills, and they also help individuals with learning disabilities increase their independence. Occupational therapy assistants work under the supervision of a registered occupational therapist (OTR) in a variety of tasks and functions, which are described below.

Do not confuse the occupational therapy assistant with the occupational therapy aide. Similar to the difference between the two types of physical therapy paraprofessional positions discussed above, these two are worlds apart in terms of training and education, job duties, and pay. Occupational therapist aides are responsible for a wide range of clerical tasks, including scheduling appointments, answering the telephone, restocking or ordering depleted supplies, and filling out insurance forms or other paperwork. Aides are not licensed, so the law does not allow them to perform as wide a range of tasks as occupational therapist assistants, and they receive most of their training on the job.

Occupational therapist assistants held about 18,000 jobs in 2002. Over 30 percent of jobs for assistants were in hospitals, 23 percent were in offices of other health practitioners (which include offices of occupational therapists), and 18 percent were in nursing care facilities. The rest were primarily in community care facilities for the elderly, home health care services, individual and family services, and state government agencies.

What Occupational Therapy Assistants Do

Occupational therapist assistants help clients with rehabilitative activities and exercises outlined in a treatment plan developed in collaboration with an occupational therapist. Activities range from teaching the proper method of moving from a bed into a wheelchair to the best way to stretch and limber the muscles of the hand. Assistants monitor an individual's activities to make sure that they are performed correctly and to provide encouragement. They also record their client's progress for the occupational therapist. If the treatment is not having the intended effect, or the client is not improving as expected, the therapist may alter the treatment program in hopes of obtaining better results. In addition, occupational therapist assistants document the billing of the client's health insurance provider. Because they work with such a broad range of patients and illnesses and disabilities, occupational therapy assistants must be able to handle a broad range of tasks. Some of these include:

- Helping a patient to handle self-care tasks such as dressing, eating, washing, and grooming
- Working with patients to prepare for job interviews or to attain the tools or skills they need for employment
- Helping make splints, braces, and other devices and maintaining tools and equipment
- Planning group or individual projects to help patients become independent to the greatest degree possible consistent with their achieving personal satisfaction
- Assisting in client evaluation

Although there are no official specialties in this field, occupational therapy assistants may end up working primarily with patients with certain kinds of disabilities, such as stroke, arthritis, diabetes, and so forth.

Training and Education

To qualify for employment in this field, applicants must be a graduate of an educational training program for assistants accredited by the American Occupational Therapy Association (AOTA) and then pass a national certification examination. Programs are offered at colleges and universities and at vocational, technical, and community colleges throughout the United States. There are no on-the-job training programs. An associate degree or a certificate from an accredited community college or technical school is generally required to qualify for occupational therapist assistant jobs.

There were 161 accredited occupational therapist assistant programs in 2003. (See the AOTA's website for a complete list of accredited schools at aota.org.) The first year of study in a typical program involves an introduction to health care, basic medical terminology, anatomy, and physiology. In the second year, courses are more rigorous and usually include occupational therapist courses in areas such as mental health, adult physical disabilities, gerontology, and pediatrics. Students also must complete sixteen weeks of supervised fieldwork in a clinic or community setting.

In planning a career as an occupational therapy assistant, besides taking courses in biology in high school, it is helpful to acquire work experience as a volunteer in a health field. Schools look favorably on this kind of experience. Since educational requirements vary from school to school, write for specific entrance information from the school or schools of interest.

Licensing and Certification

Upon completion of an accredited program, you must, as an entry-level certified occupational therapy assistant (COTA) applicant, pass a national certification examination administered by the National Board for Certification of Occupational Therapy (nbcot.org). Recertification rules for this field are fairly strict in that occupational therapy assistants must be recertified every three years and they must accumulate a certain number of professional development "units" every three years to even be eligible to take the tests. See the NBCOT website for more information.

Earnings

According to the Bureau of Labor Statistics, median annual earnings of occupational therapist assistants were $36,660 in 2002. The middle 50 percent earned between $31,090 and $43,030. The lowest 10 percent earned less than $25,600, and the highest 10 percent earned more than $48,480.

Job Outlook

According to the Bureau of Labor Statistics, occupational therapists and occupational therapy assistants are projected to be among the ten fastest-growing occupations through 2012. Because the total number of people employed is small, openings will be restricted, but certified assistants should have no trouble finding employment at least for the foreseeable future. The impact of proposed federal legislation imposing limits on reimbursement for therapy services may also adversely affect the job market for occupational therapist assistants in the near term. However, over the long run, demand for occupational therapist assistants and aides will continue to rise, due to growth in the number of individuals with disabilities or limited function. Growth will result not only from the coming of age of the baby boomers, but also because advances in medicine will allow more people with critical disabilities and injuries to survive and to need rehabilitative therapy. Third-party payers concerned with rising health care costs are expected to encourage occupational therapists to delegate more hands-on therapy work to occupational therapist assistants and aides. By having assistants and aides work more closely with clients under the guidance of a therapist, the cost of therapy should decline.

11

PARAPROFESSIONALS IN PSYCHIATRY

IN THE PRECEDING chapters, we have focused on those paraprofessionals concerned primarily with a person's physical or emotional health. But equally important, from the standpoint of the individual's total health picture, is mental health, which affects almost every aspect of our lives: how we react to stress, how we deal with people, and even our physical health and well-being. In fact, studies have shown that your mental health can greatly affect your physical health and well-being. To illustrate how mental health affects qualify of life, you need only consider that if you are constantly being disrupted or upset by feelings of guilt, anger, depression, and fear, you obviously cannot function as well as a healthy, productive human being. In this chapter we focus on paraprofessionals who help patients with mental health problems attain a higher quality of life.

In mental health, the kinds of treatment called for depend to a large degree on the severity of the illness or the person's inability to function. For the more severe mental illnesses, the services of various mental health professionals—psychiatrists and psychologists, psychiatric social workers and psychiatric registered nurses—are called for. Such professionals, who often have eight or more years of postcollege training, are qualified to handle the more complex forms of mental illness.

According to the American Psychiatric Association, nearly forty-one million persons will suffer a diagnosable mental disorder ranging from mild depression to crippling schizophrenia, and an additional eleven million will experience a substance use disorder. Psychiatrists are one kind of mental health professional whose job it is to diagnose and treat these disorders. They assess and treat mental illnesses through a combination of psychotherapy, psychoanalysis, hospitalization, and medication. Psychotherapy involves regular discussions with patients about their problems; the psychiatrist helps them find solutions through changes in their behavioral patterns, the exploration of their past experiences, and group and family therapy sessions. Psychoanalysis involves long-term psychotherapy and counseling for patients. In many cases, medications are administered to correct chemical imbalances that may be causing emotional problems. Psychiatrists may also administer electroconvulsive therapy to patients who do not respond to, or who cannot take, medications. Psychiatric technicians work with psychiatrists, helping to put into effect mental health plans and helping diagnose and observe the progress of those with mental health problems. Psychiatric technicians are also known as mental health technicians and psychiatric assistants or aides.

Psychiatric Technician

Nationally, there are approximately sixty thousand psychiatric technicians working mainly in hospitals and for state and local government mental health agencies. Psychiatric technicians should not be confused with psychiatric assistants or aides, who may perform some of the same duties and will be discussed later in this chapter. In general, psychiatric technicians receive more extensive training and are qualified to assume greater responsibilities than a psychiatric assistant.

The specific services and functions of psychiatric technicians are part of a broad treatment plan worked out by the supervising psychiatrist and other mental health professionals. Psychiatric technicians participate both in the planning and implementing of individual patient treatment plans.

Although most psychiatric technicians serve as generalists in this career, there are opportunities to specialize in certain areas of mental health care. Some choose to work with mentally disturbed children, as a counselor in a drug or alcohol abuse program, or as a member of a psychiatric emergency or crisis intervention team. In a community health clinic, technicians might work with victims of drug or alcohol abuse, parental abuse, or working with the elderly. With some training modification, psychiatric technicians might specialize in the treatment of the developmentally delayed.

What Psychiatric Technicians Do

The duties of a psychiatric technician vary depending on the work setting, but assignments may include helping patients with hygiene and housekeeping and recording patients' pulse, temperature, and respiration. Often they are called on to take part in treatment programs in a one-to-one session with patients under a nurse's or counselor's supervision; record observations of patients' behavior for other members of the mental health team; fill out admitting forms for new patients; contact patients' families for conferences; and issue medications from the pharmacy. In addition to these functions, duties of a psychiatric technician include administering oral medications and hypodermic injections and intervening to restrain violent or potentially violent or suicidal patients either by ordering them to desist or by taking whatever physical action is required.

Specific duties in a hospital unit may include most of the following tasks:

- Admitting, screening, evaluating, and discharging patients
- Interviewing and gathering information for the patient's records
- Participating in individual and group counseling and therapy sessions
- Referring patients to community agencies
- Visiting patients in their homes after they are discharged
- Handling recordkeeping
- Working with patients in behavior modification and development of social skills
- Observing various aspects of patients' lives, including eating, sleeping, and personal hygiene

Clinics, halfway houses or transitional facilities, or community mental health centers are other areas of employment for psychiatric technicians. In these establishments, duties might also include some that are unique to these settings, such as:

- Interviewing newly registered patients and their families
- Visiting patients and families at home
- Participating in group activities
- Administering psychological tests
- Reviewing patients' progress for supervising psychiatrists and other mental health professionals

Training and Education

At the very least, a high school diploma is required to find work as a psychiatric technician. Most often, however, psychiatric technicians are required to have two years of post–high school training, graduating with an associate's degree. A bachelor's degree is required by very few employers. In high school, useful courses to take to prepare you for success on the job and in continuing education include English, biology, psychology, and sociology.

Two-year associate degree programs are offered under various labels depending on their emphasis. Many are categorized as human service programs because their graduates, though they might be considered psychiatric technicians, are qualified to work with the mentally ill in various settings, all of which provide human services.

Courses of study include human development, the nature of mental illness, personality structure, and, to a limited degree, anatomy, physiology, basic nursing, and medical science. Other subjects frequently offered include an introduction to basic social sciences such as sociology and anthropology, to give you a better understanding of family and community structure; an overview of the structure and function of institutions that treat patients; and practical training to familiarize you with the skills that you will need in this field. Practical training involves providing direct patient care in an inpatient or outpatient mental health facility.

On the average, most programs are divided into four main parts. They include: (1) basic sciences; (2) general liberal arts courses, such as English, sociology, and psychology, including courses in mental-health-related topics, such as family and social welfare institutions, early childhood development, and general and abnormal psychology; (3) specific areas of study such as psychopathology, prevention techniques, forms of therapy and rehabilitation, and general and psychiatric nursing; and (4) practical and field learning experiences working directly with patients.

Licensing and Certification

Psychiatric technicians in Colorado, California, Kansas, and Arkansas must be licensed to work in this field. In these states, you must have completed a state-approved psychiatric training program to be eligible for licensure. Some states offer licensure in specific areas. In Colorado, for example, psychiatric technicians can be licensed in either care of the developmentally disabled or care of the mentally ill, depending on which kind of educational program was completed.

Although currently only a few states require certification, the trend is moving toward requiring it in more and more states. Therefore, would-be psychiatric technicians are urged to obtain certification even if it is still optional in their state. There are four levels of certification, each with increasingly higher requirements. At level one, you must have a high school diploma and pass a written examination. For certification at level two, you must have thirty semester hours of credit, a year's practical experience, and pass a written test. For level three certification, you must have an associate's degree, two years of practical experience, and pass a written exam. Finally, for level four certification, you must have a bachelor's degree, three years of experience, and again pass a written exam. More information can be found on the website of the American Association of Psychiatric Technicians at psych-health.com/aapt 01.htm.

Earnings

According to the American Association of Psychiatric Technicians, most technicians are paid by the hour. Earnings in this field ranged from $8 to $16 per hour, with the average being $12.50. With increased experience, you can expect some modest increase in salary; some senior psychiatric technicians earn as much as $27,000 per year. Salaries vary according to geographical area, level of education and experience, and work setting, with earnings the highest in California and working in a state mental hospital.

In most cases, psychiatric technicians can expect to receive some fringe benefits, including hospitalization insurance, sick leave, and paid vacations.

Job Outlook

The employment outlook for psychiatric technicians is fairly good, due primarily to two factors: There is an increasingly strong trend to return hospitalized patients to their homes following ever-increasingly shorter hospital stays. This in turn has encouraged development of comprehensive community mental health centers and boosted the need for trained psychiatric technicians. Then, too, increasing concerns over ever-accelerating health care costs should increase job opportunities in this field since psychiatric technicians can assume many of the functions of higher-paid professionals. That said, this is a relatively small field, so there are not as many jobs available as in other areas of health care.

Psychiatric Assistant

Psychiatric assistants, also known as mental health assistants or psychiatric nursing assistants or aides, provide basic care for mentally impaired or emotionally disturbed individuals. They work under a team that may include psychiatrists, psychologists, psychiatric nurses, social workers, and therapists.

More than half of all psychiatric assistants work in hospitals, primarily in psychiatric and substance abuse hospitals—although some work in the psychiatric units of general medical and surgical hospitals. Others are employed in state government agencies; residential mental retardation, mental health, and substance abuse facilities; individual and family services; and outpatient care centers. There is a tremendous amount of flexibility in terms of working hours in this job; psychiatric assistants can work days, evenings, nights, and full- or part-time.

Psychiatric assistants are often on their feet for long periods of time. The nature of the job requires that they be alert and aware at all times, be able to quickly assess the nature of a problem and come up with a solution, be calm and contained at all times, and be able to restrain patients if they become out of control. In addition, psychiatric assistants must possess strong reasoning skills and be able to persuade patients to choose less harmful behaviors if the situation calls for it.

What Psychiatric Assistants Do

As mentioned above, psychiatric assistants provide basic care for those with mental health problems. In addition to helping patients dress, bathe, groom, and eat, psychiatric assistants socialize with and lead patients in educational and recreational activities. Because they have such close contact with patients, psychiatric assistants can have a great deal of influence on their patients' outlook and treatment. In addition, psychiatric assistants do the following:

- Play games such as cards and watch television with patients
- Participate in group activities, such as sports or field trips
- Observe patients and report any physical or behavioral signs that might be important for the professional staff to know
- Accompany patients to and from examinations and treatment

Training and Education

For work in this area, usually a high school diploma or GED is sufficient, although some states require psychiatric assistants to complete a formal training program. These programs are available through professional technical schools and two-year colleges. High school classes to take in preparation for a job in this field include health, math, English, science, biology, and psychology.

Most psychiatric assistants, however, learn their skills on the job from experienced workers. During training, psychiatric assistants learn how to care for patients, read and record vital signs, and transfer or move patients safely. Volunteering in a hospital provides good experience for this occupation.

Psychiatric assistants may advance up the career ladder to psychiatric technicians following additional education. Some, in turn, choose to change jobs to that of a medical assistant, a lateral career move. In general, however, there is no room for advancement without additional education.

Licensing and Certification

There are generally no licensing and certification requirements for working as a psychiatric assistant or aide. A few states, such as California, as a condition of employment require that psychiatric assistants have a valid certified nurse assistant certificate issued by the Department of Health Services. Nurse assistant certification requires successful completion of a state-approved program; 100 hours of supervised clinical training; fifty hours of classroom training; a passing score on the written federal exam; and a criminal background check.

Earnings

According to the Bureau of Labor Statistics, median hourly earnings of psychiatric assistants were $11.04 in 2002. The middle 50 percent earned between $8.97 and $13.74 an hour. The lowest 10 percent earned less than $7.52, and the highest 10 percent earned more than $16.16 an hour. Median hourly earnings in the industries employing the largest numbers of psychiatric assistants in 2002 were as follows:

State government	$13.14
Psychiatric and substance abuse hospitals	$11.32
General medical and surgical hospitals	$11.04

Job Outlook

The number of jobs for psychiatric assistants in hospitals, where half of those in the occupation work, will grow slower than the average due to attempts to contain costs by limiting inpatient psychiatric treatment. Employment in other sectors will rise in response to growth in the number of older persons, many of whom will require mental health services, thus increasing public acceptance of formal treatment for substance abuse and lessening the stigma attached to those receiving mental health care.

12

THE FUTURE OF ALLIED HEALTH PARAPROFESSIONAL CAREERS

IN GENERAL, AS has been shown throughout this book, jobs for allied health paraprofessionals are expected to increase much more sharply than is true of the population as a whole. Because of the strong demand for personnel trained as health care paraprofessionals, the past thirty-five years have witnessed a huge growth in the number of those employed.

In just a few decades, the number of paraprofessionals has gone from a small band of paramedics and largely untrained physician assistants to an army hundreds of thousands strong—medical assistants alone account for more than two hundred thousand allied health paraprofessionals. In addition, there are more than sixty fields in which paraprofessionals are employed. Most of these new fields now have their own professional associations and standards for licensure and certification, which are required in many states, as well as standards for accreditation of training programs.

Despite this vast expansion, predicting the trends in allied health careers for the next thirty years in areas such as training, licensure, certification, and employment is risky. Even so, it seems fairly certain that for the next decade or so, opportunities for paraprofessionals will be especially promising, for reasons listed below.

Employment Opportunities

Employment in the health services field in general has never looked more promising and it will continue to grow for several reasons. As we've discussed, the number of people in older age groups, with much greater than average health care needs, will grow faster than the total population between 2002 and 2012, increasing the demand for health services, especially home health care and nursing and residential care. Advances in medical technology will continue to improve the survival rate of severely ill and injured patients, who will then need extensive therapy and care. New technologies will enable conditions not previously treatable to be identified and treated. Medical group practices and integrated health systems will become larger and more complex, thus increasing the need for office and administrative support workers. Also contributing to industry growth will be the shift from inpatient to less-expensive outpatient care, made possible by technological improvements and consumers' increasing awareness of, and emphasis on, all aspects of health. All these factors will ensure robust growth in this massive, diverse industry.

According to the Bureau of Labor Statistics, employment growth in the hospital segment is predicted to be the slowest within the health services industry. This is largely a result of efforts to control hospital costs and of the increasing emphasis on outpatient clinics and other alternative care sites. Hospitals will streamline health services delivery operations, provide more outpatient care, and rely less on inpatient care. Job opportunities, however, will remain plentiful because hospitals employ a large number of people. Besides job openings due to employment growth, additional openings will arise as workers leave the labor force or transfer to other occupations.

Occupations with the most replacement openings are usually large, with high turnover stemming from low pay and status, poor benefits, low training requirements, and a high proportion of young and part-time workers, such as nursing, psychiatric, and home health aides. By contrast, occupations with relatively few replacement openings (such as physicians and surgeons) are characterized by high pay and status, lengthy training requirements, and a high proportion of full-time workers.

Fast growth is expected for workers in occupations concentrated outside the inpatient hospital sector, such as medical assistants and home health aides. Because of cost pressures, many health services facilities will adjust their staffing patterns to reduce labor costs. Where patient care demands and regulations allow, health services facilities will substitute lower-paid providers and will cross-train their workforces. Many facilities have cut the number of middle managers, while simultaneously creating new managerial positions as they diversify. Because traditional inpatient hospital positions are no longer the only option for many future health services workers, persons seeking a career in the field must be willing to work in various employment settings.

In particular, demand for dental care will rise due to population growth, greater retention of natural teeth by middle-aged and older persons, greater awareness of the importance of dental care, and an increased ability to pay for services. Dentists will use support personnel such as dental hygienists and assistants to help meet their increased workloads.

The Department of Labor lists paraprofessional careers such as dental assistants and dental hygienists, emergency medical technicians, medical assistants, occupational therapy assistants, and physical therapist assistants among the fastest-growing occupations and those anticipated to show the greatest numerical increase in employment by 2006. For example, physical therapist assistants are expected to show an 82 percent increase in the number of those employed, followed by occupational therapy assistants with a 70 percent increase, medical assistants with an increase of approximately 59 percent, dental hygienists with a 45 percent increase, physician assistants with a 49 percent increase, and home health aides with a 48 percent increase.

Wage and salary levels in the health services industry are also projected to increase, as much as 28 percent through 2012, compared with 16 percent for all other industries combined. Employment growth is expected to account for about 3.5 million new wage and salary jobs—16 percent of all wage and salary jobs added to the economy over the 2002–12 period. Projected rates of employment growth for the various segments of the industry range from 12.8 percent in hospitals, the largest and slowest-growing industry segment, to 55.8 percent in the much smaller home health care services.

Training and Education

As the paraprofessional career fields become more established, training programs are expected to become more professionalized to ensure that graduates meet the required standards. Increasingly, training programs in many paraprofessional fields are becoming lengthier, and they are being offered in academic settings, such as universities and colleges, rather than as part of hospital training and vocational programs. Recall that many of the careers discussed in this book offered a variety of training and education options. Even within a single career path, prospective students could choose between technical/vocational, associate's degree, and bachelor's degree education. The trend is moving toward employers demanding greater levels of education from their applicants.

Accompanying this increase in standards of training programs is an increase in the standards for certification or licensing required by professional organizations and state licensing boards for those who pursue paraprofessional careers. Increasingly coming into play are new and more demanding standards for continuing education as a means of remaining accredited, with some careers demanding recertification every two or three years as well as a minimum number of hours per year working in the field. Such continuing education standards are being developed and updated in many paraprofessional fields as a means of keeping personnel up to par, thus ensuring greater job performance and patient protection. This trend for higher standards of continuing education can be expected to grow in the near future.

The overall effect of these trends may result in paraprofessionals who are better trained, able to take on new and greater responsibilities, and eligible to receive an increase in compensation.

Paraprofessional Versatility in Demand

This recognition of the importance of increased skills and capabilities has in recent years seen a corresponding trend toward graduating paraprofessionals with skills in more than one area.

Although this trend is perhaps more marked in technological fields than in the allied health area, there is nevertheless a definite trend toward more specialization and versatility. To keep hospital costs down while providing quality health care services, hospitals and other health care providers (group clinics, group practices, and medical centers, among others) are looking to paraprofessionals to handle an ever-expanding variety of primary care and secondary functions. This new emphasis will in turn result in training programs more attuned to providing students with skills that enable them to handle newer and expanded duties. In addition, this should result in greater numbers of specialized certifications, both those required by employers and optional.

Additional Information

For further information on careers covered in this book as well as many other exciting allied health and medical careers, consult the 2004–2005 edition of the AMA's *Health Professions Career and Education Directory*, which includes information on 6,500 educational programs in sixty-four different professions such as clinical assisting, dance therapy, massage therapy, and surgical assisting. Descriptions of educational programs span the forty-seven most prominent health care fields. This nearly 600-page directory contains all of the information you will need to choose the program that is right for you, including contact names and numbers, educational and admissions standards, tuition, and salary and occupational outlooks for the various professions. It costs about $65. To obtain a copy, contact:

American Medical Association
Medical Education Products
515 North State Street
Chicago, Illinois 60610
(800) 621-8335
https://catalog.ama-assn.org/catalog

For a complete list of allied health schools across the country, go to allalliedhealthschools.com.

APPENDIX

Associations and Organizations

THE ASSOCIATIONS AND organizations listed here are excellent sources of information about the variety of paraprofessional careers available in health care. They will also provide details regarding certification and licensure in any particular field.

Accreditation Review Commission on the Education for the
    Physician Assistant
12000 Findley Rd., Ste. 240
Duluth, GA 30097
arc-pa.org

Accrediting Bureau of Health Education Schools
7777 Leesburg Pike, Ste. 314 N
Falls Church, VA 22043
abhes.org

American Association of Certified Orthoptics
3914 Nakoma Rd.
Madison, WI 53711
orthoptics.org

American Association of Medical Assistants
20 N. Wacker Dr., Ste. 1575
Chicago, IL 60606
aama-ntl.org

American Association of Psychiatric Technicians
2000 O St., Ste. 250
Sacramento, CA 95814-5286
psych-health.com/aapt01.htm

American Association of Surgical Physician Assistants
4267 NW Federal Highway
PMB 201
Jensen Beach, FL 34957
aaspa.com

American Dental Assistants Association (ADAA)
35 E. Wacker Dr., Ste. 1730
Chicago, IL 60601
dentalassistant.org

American Dental Association
211 E. Chicago Ave.
Chicago, IL 60611
ada.org

American Dental Hygienists Association (ADHA)
444 N. Michigan Ave., Ste. 3400
Chicago, IL 60611
adha.org

American Medical Association
515 N. State St.
Chicago, IL 60610
ama-assn.org

American Medical Technologists
70 Higgins Rd.
Park Ridge, IL 60068
amt1.com

American Nurses Association
American Nurses Credentialing Center
600 Maryland Ave. SW, Ste. 100 West
Washington, DC 20024
http://nursingworld.org

American Occupational Therapy Association
4720 Montgomery La.
Bethesda, MD 20824
aota.org

American Optometric Association
243 N. Lindbergh Blvd.
St. Louis, MO 63141
aoa.org

American Physical Therapy Association
1111 N. Fairfax St.
Alexandria, VA 22314-1488
apta.org

American Psychiatric Association
1000 Wilson Blvd., Ste. 1825
Arlington, VA 22209-3901
psych.org

American Society for Clinical Pathology
2100 W. Harrison St.
Chicago, IL 60612
ascp.org

American Society of Podiatric Medical Assistants
2124 S. Austin Blvd.
Cicero, IL 60804
aspma.org

American Student Dental Association
211 E. Chicago Ave., Ste. 1160
Chicago, IL 60611
asdanet.org

Association of Family Practice Physician Assistants
P.O. Box 701461
San Antonio, TX 78270
afppa.org

Association of Physician Assistant Programs
950 N. Washington St.
Alexandria, VA 22314-1552
apap.org

Association of Schools for Allied Health Professions
1730 M St. NW, Ste. 500
Washington, DC 20036
asahp.org

Association of Technical Personnel in Ophthalmology
2025 Woodlane Dr.
St. Paul, MN 55125
atpo.org

Bureau of Health Professions
U.S. Department of Health and Human Services
Parklawn Bldg.
5600 Fishers La.
Rockville, MD 20857
http://bhpr.hrsa.gov

Commission on Accreditation of Allied Health Education Programs
35 E. Wacker Dr., Ste. 1970
Chicago, IL 60601
caahep.org

Commission on Dental Accreditation
211 E. Chicago Ave.
Chicago, IL 60611
ada.org/prof/ed/accred/commission/index.asp

Dental Assisting National Board
676 N. St. Clair, Ste. 1880
Chicago, IL 60611
dentalassisting.com

Joint Commission on Allied Health Personnel in Ophthalmology
2025 Woodlane Dr.
St. Paul, MN 55125
jcahpo.org

National Association of Dental Laboratories
1530 Metropolitan Blvd.
Tallahassee, FL 32308
nadl.org

National Association of Emergency Medical Technicians
P.O. Box 1400
Clinton, MS 39060
naemt.org

National Association for Home Care and Hospice
228 Seventh St. SE
Washington, DC 20003
nahc.org

National Association for Practical Nurse Education and Service
8607 Second Ave., Ste. 404A
Silver Spring, MD 20910
napnes.org

National Board for Certification in Dental Laboratory Technology
8201 Greensboro Dr., Ste. 300
McLean, VA 22102
nadl.org

National Board for Certification in Occupational Therapy
The Eugene B. Casey Bldg.
800 S. Frederick Ave., Ste. 200
Gaithersburg, MD 20877-4150
nbcot.org

National Commission on Certification of Physician Assistants
6849-B Peachtree Dunwoody Rd.
Atlanta, GA 30328
nccpa.net

National Council for State Boards of Nursing
111 E. Wacker Dr., Ste. 2900
Chicago, IL 60601
ncsbn.org

National Federation of Licensed Practical Nurses
605 Poole Dr.
Garner, NC 27529
nflpn.org

National Registry of Emergency Medical Technicians
P.O. Box 29233
Columbus, OH 43229
nremt.org

Society for Physician Assistants in Pediatrics
spap.org

Student Academy of the American Academy of Physician Assistants
http://saaapa.aapa.org

Test of English as a Second Language
Corporate Headquarters
Educational Testing Service
Rosedale Rd.
Princeton, NJ 08541
ets.org/toefl

U.S. Department of Health and Human Services
200 Independence Ave. SW
Washington, DC 20201
hhs.gov

U.S. Department of Transportation
National Highway Traffic Safety Administration
Emergency Medical Services Branch
400 Seventh Ave. SW
Washington, DC 20590
nhtsa.dot.gov

ABOUT THE AUTHOR

DR. ALEX KACEN earned his Ed.D. degree from the University of Houston in 1973 with a major in career development—career-related testing, counseling, and education. His dissertation research, which investigated career opportunities in the health field, was done in the Texas Medical Center (Houston). Before receiving his doctorate, he taught mathematics and foreign languages, his undergraduate and master's major fields. After completing his doctorate, he was a career education consultant for the state of Indiana and directed a college career testing and counseling service. Other professional activities have included serving as an external evaluator for the national career education program in Puerto Rico and developing original career-related assessment instruments used by schools, colleges, and workers representing many occupations. He has also been a member of the admissions committee of a displaced homemakers program. Dr. Kacen has published more than twenty-five articles on career development, including a book on career transitions among adults, a topic he has discussed as a featured guest on a five-part ABC television series. Dr. Kacen also acts as a management consultant to business firms—offering a wide variety of career- and employment-related workshops to such firms. He is currently the director of the Career Directions Center in San Antonio, Texas.

This edition was revised by a freelance author who specializes in writing about careers in both the liberal arts and sciences.